Pope Leo XIV

Restless Heart, Faithful Shepherd

SR. GEMMA MORATÓ SENDRA, OP

Catholic. Pastoral. Trusted.

Imprimi Potest: Kevin Zubel, CSsR, Provincial
Denver Province, The Redemptorists

Published by Liguori Publications
Liguori, Missouri 63057

Liguori Publications, a nonprofit corporation, is an apostolate of the Redemptorists (Redemptorists.com).

To order, visit Liguori.org or call 800-325-9521

Copyright © 2025 Liguori Publications

With gratitude to St. Katherine Press for their collaboration on this project.

ISBN: 978-0-7648-2900-0
E-ISBN: 978-0-7648-7280-8

Cataloging-in-Publication data has been applied for with the Library of Congress.

All rights reserved. No part of this publication may be reproduced, stored in a retrieval system, or transmitted in any form or by any means—electronic, mechanical, photocopy, recording, or any other—except for brief quotations in printed reviews, without the prior written permission of Liguori Publications.

Scripture texts in this work are taken from *The New American Bible, Revised Edition* © 2010, 1991, 1986, 1970 Confraternity of Christian Doctrine, Washington, D.C., and are used by permission of the copyright owner. All rights reserved. No part of *The New American Bible* may be reproduced in any form without permission in writing from the copyright owner.

Printed in the United States of America
29 28 27 26 25 / 5 4 3 2 1
First edition

Cover design: Wendy Barnes
Cover image of Pope Leo XIV: Stefano Speziani

Contents

Introduction: A New Era for the Church and for History   9
How Can We Be More Faithful to the Gospel?..................12
Pope Leo XIV's First *Urbi et Orbi* Blessing.........................13

Chapter 1: The Restless Heart (of an Augustinian) Who Seeks God   17
Contemplation and Mission 18
Restlessness as a Starting Point..20
Community as God's Dwelling Place...................................21
Sent on a Mission 23
Leading With the Heart of a Friar...24
Rome and Episcopal Discernment..25
A Son of Saint Augustine..26

Chapter 2: Peace Be With You!   29
Sowing Seeds of Lasting Peace..30
In the Spirit of *Fratelli Tutti*..32
A Disarmed and Disarming Peace 35

Chapter 3: God Loves Us Unconditionally   39
God Loved Us First, So That We Might Love Him 40
Come and See—Let Us Come to Know Jesus Christ........41
The Lord Himself Comes to Meet Us..................................42
Suffering Can Lead to Revelation 45
Dreaming Together..46

Chapter 4: Evil Will Not Prevail — 49
A Prophetic Declaration 50
Christian Courage 51
We Are Not Alone 52
In His Hands 54
Sustained by a Faithful Love 55

Chapter 5: Jesus, the Good Shepherd — 57
A Pastoral Style 58
Jesus Never Abandons His Flock 60
The Good Shepherd Lays Down His Life for the Sheep 62

Chapter 6: To Be Missionaries — 65
The Gospel Is Proclaimed With Boldness 66
Social Justice and Human Rights 70
Attention to the Peripheries 71
Without Fear 73
Always a Missionary 75

Chapter 7: A Synodal Church — 79
Communion, Listening, and Conversion 80
Episcopal Leadership 82
Polarization—A Sign of Deeper Wounds? 83

Chapter 8: A United Church — 87
A Brother Among Brothers 88
Living in Communion 90

Chapter 9: A Church That Builds Bridges — 93

Between the Human and the Divine 94
Recognizing One Another as Brothers and Sisters 95
To Heal, to Share, to Grow, to Be Enlightened 97
Church Called to Be Home 99

Chapter 10: Mary Walks With Us — 101

Filial Trust 102
Mary Inspires Discipleship 103
Mary and Synodality 104
The Pope Entrusts Himself to Mary 105

Conclusion: A Pontificate With Roots and a Future — 107

About the Author — 111

Annuntio vobis gaudium magnum;
habemus Papam:
Eminentissimum ac Reverendissimum
Dominum
Robertum Franciscum
Sanctae Romanae Ecclesiae
Cardinalem Prevost
qui sibi nomen imposuit Leo XIV.

I announce to you a great joy;
we have a Pope:
The Most Eminent and Most Reverend Lord
Robert Francis Cardinal Prevost
of the Holy Roman Church
who has taken the name Leo XIV.

Introduction

A New Era for the Church and for History

There are people whose presence doesn't impose, but transforms. These people don't seek the spotlight, yet they "illuminate," as St. Thomas Aquinas once said. They don't raise their voices, yet they leave a lasting impression. They walk quietly behind the scenes, without a desire for prominence, yet they are often the soul behind key decisions—the whisper that orients; the listener who sustains.

Such has been the path of Robert Francis Prevost for decades: Augustinian friar, missionary in distant lands, bishop among the poor, prefect entrusted with discerning and appointing pastors throughout the world, and now Successor of Peter under the name Leo XIV. Yet, above all, he has been a seeker: a tireless seeker of truth in the spirit of St. Augustine, his spiritual teacher. Like St. Augustine, bishop of Hippo, Prevost has understood the Christian life as an interior journey of constant searching—sustained by faith and nourished by prayer, study, and community.

His vocation was not born of strategy or calculation,

but of that restlessness of heart to which Augustine gave immortal expression: "You have made us for yourself, O Lord, and our heart is restless until it rests in you." For St. Augustine and for Prevost, truth is not an abstract concept or intellectual construction, but a living person: Jesus Christ.

Following the Augustinian spirit, Prevost never felt the need to defend truth but to proclaim it with his life and let it speak for itself. As St. Augustine famously said, "The truth is like a lion. You don't have to defend it. Let it loose. It will defend itself." This radical trust in the power of the gospel has shaped Prevost's style: humble yet firm, quiet yet courageous.

Robert Francis Prevost—now Pope Leo XIV—is a man who avoids rigid formulas and easy certainties. He is a shepherd who walks with seekers, unafraid of their questions and patient in accompaniment. For he knows, with Augustine, that only someone who has sincerely searched can help others to find. And that truth, once found, liberates, transforms, and sends forth.

Leo XIV's life has not been an ecclesiastical climb to the top, but a pastoral path marked by service, empathy, and quiet fidelity. He never sought to stand out, yet he was chosen for one of the most demanding roles on earth. And he accepted it with the simplicity of someone who did not pursue the position, but who responds to a call. For him, as for many before him, service is not ambition, but—in the way of Jesus—a form of love.

From a young age, Robert Prevost responded generously to God's call to live in fraternity, embracing communal life as an Augustinian friar. He held a deep intuition that God is best sought and found in community, as Augustinian spirituality teaches. He understood that Christian life cannot be lived in isolation; it is lived in shared bread, shared faith, shared questions, and shared dreams with fellow seekers of God.

The Augustinian charism is not a romanticized ideal; it is a concrete way of following Christ by living in unity, "with one heart and one soul directed toward God," as *The Rule of Saint Augustine* expresses. This choice, made in youth and sustained over the years, formed Leo XIV's pastoral heart and has proven to be the foundation of his style as pope: humble, fraternal, engaged in dialogue, and always open to walking with others.

From the moment he stepped onto the central balcony of Saint Peter's Basilica after the eagerly awaited "*habemus Papam,*" we could tell that the new pope had much to say. And he did not speak with pomp or solemn proclamations, but with humble signs that spoke more deeply than any speech. His reverent silence, serene gaze, restrained emotion, and delicate gestures—and that quiet gulp to hold back tears—spoke volumes. Leo XIV wasn't just beginning a new pontificate; he was initiating a new chapter in the Church and in history.

In those first moments, the hallmarks of the Pope's style were already clear: humility without artifice, closeness without condescension, service without conditions. A pontificate rooted in the logic of the gospel, not in power; of fraternity, not of privilege—all within the frame of a symbolic year: the Jubilee of Hope.

A new era began for the Church. And it began with the demeanor of one who knows that true change starts not in grand gestures, but in a heart open to the Spirit—the same way that Cardinal Robert Francis Prevost conducted himself in the conclave.

Few had imagined Prevost on the balcony in front of the crowd. Yet many, upon seeing him appear, understood that his time had come. Not because of charisma or eloquent speeches, but because he embodies something essential: traits of the Good Shepherd, who is straightforward, missionary, and full of God. Someone who brings no personal agenda; someone with the availability of a person who has learned to live in a posture of listening. His election has been a surprise of the Spirit, as so often are the most beautiful passages of the gospel.

How Can We Be More Faithful to the Gospel?

What can we do to ensure that Christ remains the center of our lives?

Pope Leo XIV said the following in his first homily:

In [Christ], God, in order to make himself close and accessible to men and women, revealed himself to us in the trusting eyes of a child, in the lively mind of a young person, and in the mature features of a man (cf. Gaudium et Spes, 22), finally appearing to his disciples after the resurrection with his glorified body. He thus showed us a model of human holiness that we can all imitate, together with the promise of an eternal destiny that transcends all our limits and abilities.

In this same spirit, Leo XIV invites us to live a faith that is incarnate, alive, and open to the world and to others—a faith that neither retreats nor hides but becomes proposal, testimony, and encounter.

Over the course of ten chapters, we will explore key themes inspired by the message Pope Leo read—not improvised—with his first *Urbi et Orbi* blessing as Peter's successor. As if wishing to leave nothing essential unsaid at such a meaningful moment, Leo XIV revealed his intent with the simple gesture of bringing a sheet of paper in hand so that he could offer from the start a message that was well thought out, prayed about, and deliberate. He did not seek the emotional impact of spontaneity but the clarity of a well-considered message to set the tone—serene, pastoral, and forward-looking—for his pontificate.

This book is not a theoretical analysis; it is a spiritual and ecclesial meditation on the pontificate that is unfolding and an opportunity to know the man who now wears the fisherman's sandals. A new time has indeed begun. And the Lord, as always, invites us to walk forward in trust.

Pope Leo XIV's First *Urbi et Orbi* Blessing

On the afternoon of May 8, 2025, the newly elected Holy Father, Pope Leo XIV, preceded by the cross, appeared on Saint Peter's Basilica's central balcony—called the Loggia of the Blessings—to greet the people and impart his first *Urbi et Orbi* (which means "To the city [of Rome] and to the world) papal blessing. Before the solemn blessing, the new Pope addressed the faithful with the following words:

Peace be with you all!

Dear brothers and sisters, these are the first words spoken by the risen Christ, the Good Shepherd who laid down his life for God's flock. I would like this greeting of peace to resound in your hearts, in your families, among all people, wherever they may be, in every nation and throughout the world. Peace be with you!

This is the peace of the risen Christ. A peace that is unarmed and disarming, humble and persevering. A peace that comes from God, the God who loves us all unconditionally.

We can still hear the faint yet ever-courageous voice of Pope Francis as he blessed Rome, the Pope who blessed Rome, who gave his blessing to the world, the whole world, on the morning of Easter. Allow me to extend that same blessing: God loves us, God loves you all, and evil will not prevail! All of us are in God's hands. So, let us move forward, without fear, together, hand in hand with God and with one another! We are followers of Christ. Christ goes before us. The world needs his light. Humanity needs him as the bridge that can lead us to God and his love. Help us, one and all, to build bridges through dialogue and encounter, joining together as one people, always at peace. Thank you, Pope Francis!

I also thank my brother cardinals, who have chosen me to be the Successor of Peter and to walk together with you as a Church, united, ever pursuing peace and justice, ever seeking to act as men and women faithful to Jesus Christ, in order to proclaim the gospel without fear, to be missionaries.

I am an Augustinian, a son of St. Augustine, who once said, "For you, I am a bishop; with you, I am a Christian." In this sense, all of us can journey together toward the homeland that God has prepared for us.

A special greeting to the Church of Rome! Together, we must look for ways to be a missionary Church, a Church that builds bridges and encourages dialogue, a Church ever open to welcoming, like this square with its open arms, all those who are in need of our charity, our presence, our readiness to dialogue and our love.

(In Spanish)

Y si me permiten también una palabra, un saludo a todos y en modo particular a mi querida diócesis de Chiclayo, en el Perú, donde un pueblo fiel ha acompañado a su obispo, ha compartido su fe y ha dado tanto, tanto, para seguir siendo Iglesia fiel de Jesucristo.

(Translation)

And if you also allow me a brief word, a greeting to everyone and in particular to my beloved Diocese of Chiclayo, in Peru, where a faithful people has accompanied its bishop, shared its faith, and given so much, so much, to continue being a faithful Church of Jesus Christ.

To all of you, brothers and sisters in Rome, in Italy, throughout the world: we want to be a synodal Church, a Church that moves forward, a Church that always seeks peace, that always seeks charity, that always seeks to be close above all to those who are suffering.

Today is the day of the Prayer of Supplication to Our Lady of Pompeii. Our Mother Mary always wants to walk at our side, to remain close to us, to help us with her intercession and her love. So, I would like to pray together with you. Let us pray together for this new mission, for the whole Church, for peace in the world, and let us ask Mary, our Mother, for this special grace: Hail Mary....

Chapter 1

The Restless Heart (of an Augustinian) Who Seeks God

*"But whoever is made to suffer
as a Christian should not be ashamed
but glorify God because of the name."*
1 Peter 4:16

*"I am a son of St. Augustine, an Augustinian,
who said, 'For you, I am a bishop; with you,
I am a Christian.'"*

CONTEMPLATION AND MISSION

After Pope Francis—a Jesuit and faithful follower of St. Ignatius in both spirit and action—has come (or, rather, has been given to us by the Spirit) Pope Leo XIV, Robert Francis Prevost, another religious, this time an Augustinian friar. Being Augustinian will give his pontificate a distinct style, as he has drunk from the living waters of early Christianity.

He belongs to the Order of Saint Augustine (OSA), a mendicant order with communities located in the heart of cities, among the people, where everyday life pulses. Their presence seeks no privilege, nor does the order withdraw itself from the world; rather, it places them as witnesses in the midst of life. The friars preach where the people live, share in the people's joys and sufferings, and survive by charity, trusting in God's providence and the generosity of the faithful. Contemplation and mission are not separate dimensions, but two expressions of a single commitment: to seek God and make him present in word and service. This is the spirit in which the mendicant orders—such as the Augustinians, Franciscans, Dominicans, and Carmelites—were born.

The OSA is one of the great orders of the thirteenth century, born from a deep and ever-renewed desire to return to the gospel as a way of life, as center and horizon. They wanted to return to the gospel not in an introspective or idealized way, but in a way that was lived out in fraternal, poor, prayerful communities, in service to the people and the Church.

Although the OSA's formal constitutions as a religious order dates back to 1244—and the order was definitively unified by Pope Alexander IV in 1256—its soul is much older. It is rooted in *The Rule of Saint Augustine,* written by St. Augustine of Hippo in the fourth century for early Christians who wished to live together "with one heart and one soul directed toward God" (*una anima et cor unum in Deum*).

Saint Augustine's rule, the shortest of the four great monastic rules of the Church—alongside those of Sts. Basil, Benedict, and Albert—does not impose rigid structures or extraordinary ascetic practices. Rather, it proposes a way of life marked by fraternal charity, shared goods, common prayer, mutual obedience, and the joint search for truth. Augustinian spirituality is a way of being in the world: open to God from within; open to others in humility.

For Robert Francis Prevost, born in Chicago, Illinois, on September 14, 1955, this tradition is not merely a doctrinal framework. It is his home, his spiritual mother tongue, the air he has breathed since he entered the minor seminary of the OSA at age fourteen. He later joined the novitiate in 1977 in the Province of Our Lady of Good Counsel in St. Louis, Missouri. He made his solemn vows on August 29, 1981.

Within the order he was formed, he matured as a religious, and he has carried out all the tasks the Church has entrusted to him—from his mission in Peru to his governance of the order and his global guidance of bishops.

In an interview for an Augustinian publication, then-Cardinal Prevost was asked how St. Augustine influenced his daily life. He responded with a glimpse into how deeply the bishop of Hippo inspires his vision of the Church and of listening, discernment, and service:

> *One of the things that comes to mind when I think of St. Augustine—his vision and understanding of what it means to belong to the Church—is his teaching that you cannot say you are a follower of Christ without being part of the Church. Christ is part of the Church. He is the head. So, people who think they can follow Christ "on their own," without being part of the body, are, unfortunately, distorting what is truly an authentic experience. Saint Augustine offers wisdom that permeates everything and helps us live in communion. Unity and communion are essential charisms of the order's life and fundamental to understanding what it means to be the Church and to belong to the Church.*

As the constitutions of the order, which Leo professes and lives, affirm, faithfulness to the Church and to the supreme pontiffs is not an institutional concession, but an expression of Augustinian love for unity and truth. For Augustine, and for those who follow his path, there is no greater sign of spiritual maturity than knowing oneself to be a living member of a greater body: the body of Christ, which is the Church.

Restlessness as a Starting Point

The first chapter of St. Augustine's *Confessions* begins, "You have made us for yourself, O Lord, and our heart is restless until it rests in you." This phrase is not only the famed opening of one of the foundational works of Christian spirituality but also, above all, an existential confession, the heartbeat of a soul that seeks meaning. Generation after generation, those who have felt the call of God as a loving unrest not calmed by superficial answers or dulled by easy certainties have recognized themselves in these words. Robert Francis Prevost also recognizes himself in them, naturally and deeply. He perceived that same call not as a burden, but as a promise of fulfillment, and he lived it out by choosing life in a religious community.

Prevost did not enter the Order of Saint Augustine because of youthful impulse or passing enthusiasm. He was moved by a deeper, almost silent, intuition: the certainty that God is not found in the noise of the world nor in immediate success, but in the deepest beat of the human heart. That inner conviction led him to embrace the Augustinian spiritual tradition not as a relic of the past, but as a living, possible, and necessary path.

Community as God's Dwelling Place

From an early age, Prevost understood that the Augustinian way of life is indeed a path, but not a solitary one. It is a journey made at the pace of others, like pilgrims who do not rush, knowing that meaning lies in the path shared. The Augustinian is not an isolated monk or a lone seeker of perfection. He is, above all, a brother—a companion in the search for God. A man who builds community through truth and charity.

"There is nothing more characteristic of Augustinian

life than sharing everything: the table, prayer, doubts, and faith," Prevost once said. And that is exactly what he has done. From his first steps as a friar to his election as prior general of the order, his life has been that of a weaver of communion born from deep conviction. Patient, faithful, discreet, Prevost has lived fraternity not as an ideal, but as a concrete way of following Christ.

His way of life is the fruit of a living tradition. Constitution 13 of the Order of Saint Augustine puts it clearly:

> *The aim of the order is that, united in fraternity and spiritual friendship, we may seek and honor God and serve his people. In this way, we participate in the Church's mission of evangelization, bringing the Good News "to all human groups, so that, being transformed from within by its own power, humanity itself may be renewed." This is our primary witness.*

This paragraph describes precisely the trajectory of Pope Leo XIV. His religious life has been a constant response to that call: to seek together, to honor God with others, to serve without craving recognition. He has never separated interiority from mission, nor prayer from pastoral action. His spirituality, like Augustine's, has been incarnate: feet on the ground, heart turned toward God.

Augustine did not seek God in absolute silence, but in shared words, in Scripture read with others, in dialogue among brothers. In Robert Francis Prevost, this legacy has taken luminous and lucid form—as novice master, seminary rector, provincial prior, and later as prior general.

He has always championed a formation that integrates spiritual experience and fraternal life.

His approach has never been about strategies or rules, but about accompaniment. His way of guidance is to listen, discern, and encourage. He does not offer prefabricated answers, and he poses questions that help others seek together. Like Augustine, the man who would become pope knew that the path to truth goes through love, and that truth can only be reached when it is shared. That is the great lesson of being Augustinian: that God does not impose himself; instead, he reveals himself through experience and personal encounter, fostering a loving and reciprocal bond.

Sent on a Mission

After joining the Augustinian order, Robert Francis Prevost completed his formation at the Catholic Theological Union in Chicago. At the age of twenty-seven, he was sent to Rome to study canon law, and he earned his doctorate from the Pontifical University of St. Thomas Aquinas (Angelicum). In the Eternal City, he was ordained a priest on June 19, 1982. In 1985, while working on his doctoral thesis, he was sent to the Augustinian mission in Chulucanas, Piura, Peru, where he stayed until 1986.

At the Augustinian mission in Trujillo, Peru, Prevost ministered for eleven years, from 1988 to 1999, serving in roles including prior of the community, formation director, and instructor for professed members while also teaching at the San Carlos and San Marcelo Seminary and working with local parishes.

In Peru, he discovered a new dimension of Augustinian spirituality: insertion into the reality of the poor. In the dusty regions of Trujillo and Chulucanas, he learned that the restlessness of the heart is not calmed by ideas alone, but by commitment. "Where the people are, there the Church is," he would say. "Where there is suffering, God cries out."

Years later, he returned to Peru as bishop of Chiclayo. He reconnected with humble communities, encouraged processes of reconciliation, and promoted the formation of the clergy. He lived his pastoral ministry as a constant act of love. He did not seek grand gestures, but daily fidelity. Like a true Augustinian, he knew that God acts more through perseverance than spectacle. On the day of his election as supreme pontiff, he did not forget his people. He offered them words that stirred the hearts of many Peruvians:

And if you also allow me a brief word, a greeting to everyone and in particular to my beloved Diocese of Chiclayo, in Peru, where a faithful people has accompanied its bishop, shared its faith, and given so much, so much, to continue being a faithful Church of Jesus Christ.

This small but significant gesture revealed that, even at such an overwhelming moment, he never lost sight of the reality of his life and mission.

Leading With the Heart of a Friar

In 2001, Prevost was elected prior general of the Augustinians, a role he fulfilled for twelve years. He was called to lead the order through a time of profound change: a decline in vocations in Europe, growth in Africa and Asia, and the challenges of inculturation and mission. But he never lost his identity. He governed with the heart of a friar: listening, engaging in conversation, discerning—a leader but also an encouraging older brother.

During his term as prior general, he wrote numerous letters and messages to Augustinian communities around the world. These letters reflected a simple, profound spirituality centered on fraternal charity, truth sought in communion, and hope in the midst of difficulty. "Augustine's charism," he said, "is not a relic, but a compass. It reminds us that the Church is called to live as a community of love, not as a structure of power."

Rome and Episcopal Discernment

Pope Francis called the future pope to Rome in 2023 to preside over the Dicastery for Bishops as prefect. According to the Holy See, "The Dicastery for Bishops is responsible for all matters related to the establishment and provision of particular churches and the exercise of episcopal ministry in the Latin Church."

This appointment was meaningful: a pastor with missionary experience and the heart of a religious was to help choose the new bishops of the Church. Faithful to his spirituality, his criteria for new bishops were clear: men of prayer, of listening, of communion. He was not seeking administrators or diplomats, but witnesses to the gospel.

Prevost explained how he became prefect in a September 30, 2023, interview with the General Curia office shortly after he was named a cardinal:

The fact that Pope Francis asked me to accept this mission was a complete surprise to me. I had been part of the Dicastery for several years, since 2020, and when he told me he was "thinking about the possibility," I told the Holy Father, "You know that I'm very happy in Peru. Whether you decide to appoint me or to leave me where I am, I'll be happy. But if you ask me to take on a new role in the Church, I will accept." And that's because of my vow of obedience. I've always done what I have been asked to do, whether in the order or in the Church. And then he said, "Pray that I make a good decision." And, well...the rest is now known.

This task of appointing bishops—perhaps a quiet one—was nevertheless impactful. The Church of the coming years bears the imprint of Prevost's discernment. In his decisions, he applied an Augustinian lens: his aim was not to fill vacancies, but to raise up pastors who carry the best interests of their flock and who walk the path laid out by Pope Francis with the Word in their hands and charity in their hearts.

In this, he was faithful to St. Augustine, who became a bishop reluctantly, but never ceased to be a servant.

A Son of Saint Augustine

As we have seen, Robert Francis Prevost has never ceased to recognize himself in the footsteps of his spiritual father, St. Augustine of Hippo. He has taken on the Petrine ministry as Leo XIV from a place of humility inherited from Augustine—one that inspired the saint to say, upon becoming bishop of Hippo, "For you, I am a bishop; with you, I am a Christian" (*Pro vobis episcopus, vobiscum christianus*). After his election, Pope Leo XIV said those same words with quiet conviction—and we can be sure it was not an eloquent quote, but a declaration of identity.

His vocation is the pairing of communion and service, of shared faith and authority exercised as responsibility. There is no trace of clericalism in this vision of ministry, but the deep echo of a spirituality that places Christ at the center and allows itself to be shaped by Christ through fraternity. This is how Friar Prevost lived his path—as an Augustinian, as a pastor, and as a brother among brothers.

Saint Augustine taught that truth is sought together and lived in charity. Leo XIV, with his Augustinian formation, brings to the Church this legacy of shared interiority and pastoral wisdom.

Chapter 2

Peace Be With You!

"Though the doors were shut, Jesus came and stood among them and said, 'Peace be with you'."

John 20:26

"This is the peace of the risen Christ. A peace that is unarmed and disarming."

Sowing Seeds of Lasting Peace

Leo XIV began his Petrine ministry with the same words the risen Christ spoke to his disciples: "Peace be with you." This was no random choice, no routine liturgical phrase—it was a proclamation that encapsulated the very heart of the gospel. Jesus never tires of sending his Church as an artisan of communion into a wounded, divided, and yearning world. And such a mission—similar to the missions of St. Augustine and Leo XIV's predecessor, Pope Francis—requires reconciled hearts, open to others, ready to work for peace born of love and forged in truth.

"Peace be with you." This was not an empty expression, but a deliberate, meaningful declaration. Leo XIV's entire pastoral life has been marked by a tireless pursuit of peace—not merely as the absence of conflict, but as the fullness of life, as reconciliation, as incarnate justice, as concrete fraternity. Throughout the future Pope's journey, he has built bridges, healed rifts, and planted the seeds of a deep, evangelical, and enduring peace in the Church and the world.

As bishop of Chiclayo—who placed his beloved diocese on the map for many—he regularly shared rich and thoughtful reflections in the diocesan bulletin, *Somos Iglesia*, a true pastoral tool for the people. In one of those writings, commenting on Pope Francis's 2020 encyclical *Fratelli Tutti* (On Fraternity and Social Friendship), he revealed what might now be read as a clear declaration of intent: his decisive commitment to peace—not as abstract rhetoric or a utopian ideal, but as a tangible, spiritual, and pastoral responsibility woven into the daily life of the Church and society. Drawing from the encyclical's message, he invited the faithful to rediscover fraternity as a path, listening as a method, and mercy as a lifestyle. For him, to speak of peace was first and foremost to speak of personal, communal, and ecclesial conversion.

In his own words, Bishop Prevost emphasized, "Once again, the Pope issues a definitive 'no' to war and to globalized indifference. Fraternity and social friendship are, according to the Pope, the necessary means to reconstruct a wounded world." That vision—calm but resolute—has accompanied Robert Francis Prevost throughout each stage of his ministry; now, as he is Successor of Peter, it becomes a horizon for the entire Church.

In two brief pages of the Chiclayo diocesan bulletin, he laid out what Pope Francis, citing the Poor Man of Assisi, wanted to convey in *Fratelli Tutti*: a spiritual and social itinerary with the single goal of building a more just, more human, truly united world where peace is not merely an ideal, but a concrete, enduring reality lived in all of our relationships.

To achieve this, he insisted on something fundamental: no authentic transformation will be possible without the participation of everyone. Peace must be built together. That is why *Fratelli Tutti* is not only a message for political or religious leaders but also a call to every person of goodwill. And Bishop Prevost stressed that Pope Francis raised his voice against everything that threatens peace: war, violence, contempt for others, and globalized indifference. Community and social friendship are the two paths for rebuilding a wounded world.

He stated, "This encyclical invites us to have open hearts to work in solidarity with everyone, seeking the transformation of society and of institutions in order to build a more human, more just, more fraternal world where no one is excluded."

In the Spirit of *Fratelli Tutti*

The encyclical reveals its proposal through eight chapters, which can be read as eight stations on a path of social, spiritual, and pastoral conversion aimed at "rebuilding a wounded world." As bishop of Chiclayo, Prevost read *Fratelli Tutti* with a pastoral lens, grounded and real. He did not merely explain its content; he embodied it in his words and life. In a pastoral letter to his faithful, he walked through the encyclical with evangelical clarity and spiritual depth, highlighting several ideas:

1. Pope Francis began by realistically portraying the "dark clouds" of our time. He courageously denounced the consequences of a culture marked by selfishness, isolation, and indifference. He spoke of racism, poverty, human trafficking, inequality, exploitation, slavery, and organized crime. This is not a grim inventory, but a gospel-based diagnosis: to heal the world, we must first see its wounds. We cannot pretend nothing is wrong. Bishop Prevost made these words his own: "A Church that does not allow itself to be wounded by the pain of the world loses its credibility."

2. In the second chapter of the encyclical, Pope Francis returned to one of the most luminous parables in the gospel: the Good Samaritan, which contains an essential key for rebuilding our social fabric: becoming a neighbor. The origin or ideology of the one who suffers

does not matter. What matters is to draw near, to see, to touch, to heal. The other is not a threat or a burden, but is Christ himself, wounded on the roadside. "We must recognize Christ in every excluded person," Francis said—and Bishop Prevost wholeheartedly embraced this, convinced that a pastoral approach rooted in tenderness is the only logical response to a fractured humanity.

3. Love is the axis of the third chapter. "Love takes first place," wrote Pope Francis. To love as a life choice, as a political commitment, as a theological principle. To embrace love that welcomes instead of fear that excludes. To promote unity and the dignity of all instead of indifference. Social friendship is not superficial; it is the fabric that sustains human life. Leo XIV has repeated this again and again: the Church cannot stop loving, because she was sent to reconcile, not to condemn.

4. The encyclical then addresses one of the most painful wounds of our time: migration. Francis called us to overcome narratives of rejection or fear and proposes a culture of welcome, integration, and generosity. And he reminded us of a critical truth: "Nowadays, we are either all saved together or no one is saved." No one can be left out. No one can be discarded.

Pope Leo XIV made this equally clear in his first *Urbi et Orbi* blessing, stating in a calm and firm voice: "Peace be with you all! Dear brothers and sisters...I would like this greeting of peace to resound in your hearts, in your families, among all people, wherever they may be.... Peace be with you!"

5. Returning to *Fratelli Tutti*, Leo XIV reaffirms that charity, according to Francis, is the spiritual heart of politics. But not just any politics—politics oriented toward the common good, promoting justice and defending the least. Only from there can a true civilization of love emerge. Fraternity must influence public decisions and the responsible exercise of power. Pope Leo XIV has embraced that same vision: to govern in the Church, as in society, is to serve.

6. *Fratelli Tutti* presents an urgent call to dialogue—not violent debate or ideological imposition, but sincere encounter, mutual respect, and shared learning. "Life… is the art of encounter," Francis insisted. And dialogue becomes a path to peace because it brings perspectives closer, heals wounds, and resolves conflicts without violence.

    Peace is built when reconciliation, not revenge, is pursued. Reconciliation is not naivety, but justice transformed by forgiveness. Francis proposed a society based on service, sharing, and the pursuit of the common good. He went even further by reiterating the Church's absolute opposition to the death penalty and any punishment that denies human dignity. Leo XIV embraces this teaching with conviction, knowing that mercy is the most visible face of the gospel.

7. The encyclical ends, as the bishop of Chiclayo summarized, with a call to interreligious dialogue. Religions must not be sources of division or excuses for violence, but instruments of peace, unity, and transformation. Francis warned in a 2018 address in Riga, Latvia:

> *If the music of the gospel ceases to resonate in our very being, we will lose the joy born of compassion, the tender love born of trust, and the capacity for reconciliation that has its source in our knowledge that we have been forgiven and sent forth. If the music of the gospel ceases to sound in our homes, our public squares, our workplaces, our political and financial life, then we will no longer hear the strains that challenge us to defend the dignity of every man and woman.*

This sentiment also summarizes Leo XIV's hope that the Church never loses her music, that the melody of the gospel—born from a heart inhabited by Christ—continues to sound.

A Disarmed and Disarming Peace

"This is the peace of the risen Christ. A peace that is unarmed and disarming." With these words, charged with evangelical power, Pope Leo XIV summed up in his first *Urbi et Orbi* blessing the very core of the Christian message: the peace brought by the Lord is not imposed by force or fear, and it is not sustained by power. It is an unarmed peace because it springs from a love that gives itself without defending itself, and it is disarming because it tears down walls and neutralizes hatred.

Reflecting on Pope Francis' encyclical, Prevost insisted that such peace requires deep conversion. It is not enough to desire it or proclaim it—we must live it. And to live it means moving from "I" to "we," from fear to trust, from judgment to embrace. It is not a matter of superficial outward changes—it is about transforming hearts. It is about allowing the gospel to reach us until it reshapes our relationships, our affections, and our decisions.

For Prevost as bishop and now as Leo XIV, this was, is, and will be the Church's great challenge: to form communities where all people, without exception, can feel at home. Communities that welcome before they judge, that heal before they condemn, that go out to meet others rather than retreat into their own comforts. Churches that are open and missionary and have a Good Samaritan outlook, recognizing Christ in the other and building a common path with them.

For, as the missionary Robert Francis Prevost clearly affirms, true peace will not come from fragile agreements, provisional pacts, or cautious diplomacy. It will come only from hearts touched by the gospel. It will come from men and women who dare to live as brothers and sisters. It will come from disciples who are capable of renouncing violence, the need to dominate, and the urge to be right, embracing instead the humility of shared bread, forgiveness offered, and quiet service.

What Pope Leo XIV has sought to say—and what he has expressed more by actions than by words—is that there is no Church without communion, no communion without conversion, and no conversion without peace. And true peace disarms us, transforms us, and reveals a kingdom not of this world—yet already dwelling within us.

Leo XIV was unequivocal in his first *Regina Caeli* on Good Shepherd Sunday, May 11, 2025, saying, "I consider it a gift from God that the first Sunday of my service as bishop of Rome is Good Shepherd Sunday, the fourth

Sunday of Easter." He continued after the *Regina Caeli*: "In today's dramatic scenario of a piecemeal third world war, as Pope Francis stated many times, I too address the world's leaders, repeating the ever-timely appeal: 'Never again war!'"

He could not have said this more clearly, nor at a more fitting moment. The following day, at his first meeting with representatives of the media, Leo XIV reinforced this message, saying:

> *Peace begins with each one of us—with the way we look at others, the way we listen to others, the way we speak about others. And in this sense, the way we communicate is fundamentally important: we must say "no" to the war of words and images. We must reject the paradigm of war.*

CHAPTER 3

GOD LOVES US UNCONDITIONALLY

*"For the Father himself loves you,
because you have loved me and have come to
believe that I came from God."*

JOHN 16:27

"God loves us. God loves you all."

God Loved Us First, So That We Might Love Him

"God loves us. God loves you all." With this simple and radiant expression, Pope Leo XIV summed up the essence of the gospel. Everything begins in God's freely given love. Everything blossoms in that certainty of God's love: the foundation of Christian life. Because, as St. Augustine taught, we do not begin by loving God, but we are loved first; in knowing we are loved, we learn to love in return: "The Father himself loves you, because you have loved me."

Does God love us because we love him, or do we love him because he first loved us? The same gospel answers through its epistle. St. Augustine writes, in *In Epistolam Ioannis ad Parthos tractatus decem* (Ten Homilies on the Epistle of John to the Parthians), "We love because he first loved us. Thus, it is because we were loved that we came to love. In truth, loving God is a gift from God. He who loved us without being loved gave us the means to love Him. That there might be something in us with which to please Him, we were loved even when we were unlovable."

Love is the central message of Jesus—not as an abstract commandment, but as a concrete experience. And as the Pope reminded his faithful in Peru repeatedly, we cannot love God if we do not learn to love our neighbor. There is no true spirituality without compassion. There is no mature faith without fraternity. And, if God loves all of us, then no one can be excluded. No one is unnecessary. No one is disposable. No one is a stranger in the eyes of Christ.

During his episcopal ministry in Chiclayo—especially in the hardest months of the pandemic—Bishop Prevost wrote frequently to his communities. He did not speak from the pulpit, but he wrote from the heart. His letters and pastoral reflections were both balm and guidance. In one of them, titled with a gospel phrase, "Come and See...Let Us Come to Know Jesus Christ" (See John 1:39.), he made his conviction clear: only Christ can truly teach us how to live. It was not about sustaining structures or maintaining ecclesial routines, but returning to the center, to what is essential, to the living person of Jesus. Jesus comes to show us the true way to live.

Years later, as prefect in Rome, Prevost said, "We have often focused on teaching doctrine, but we run the risk of forgetting that our first task is to communicate the beauty and joy of knowing Jesus." Jesus, whose heart is open to all.

Come and See—
Let Us Come to Know Jesus Christ

Saint Augustine taught that truth is not imposed; it is sought. And it is not reached through isolation or power, but through communion. Augustine's life was an interior, but never closed-off, pilgrimage. Around him grew a community of seekers: brothers and sisters with whom he shared not only faith but also questions, tears, doubts, and certainties. For St. Augustine, truth was inseparable from charity, and charity inseparable from relationship. That is why he taught that only together do we arrive at the light.

In this swiftly changing world that prizes individualism, the Pope reminds us that we were created in the image and likeness of God. We were not made to live in isolation, but in community. We were made to build relationships and to inhabit society as brothers and sisters.

Leo XIV, the first Augustinian pope, is heir to this

spirit. Not only did he profess vows in the Order of Saint Augustine, but the way he lives bears the imprint of that spirituality: interiority without isolation, wisdom without arrogance, authority without harshness. In him, the Augustinian spirituality is not an ideal or a memory, but a concrete way of dwelling in the world with attentive eyes, an open heart, and feet on the ground. This is a spirituality of being alert to reality, accompanying others with compassion, and healing with hope.

Leo XIV's pastoral style does not seek to attract through grand speeches or lengthy texts, but through gestures that invite closeness, communion, and communication without fear. When the first disciples, moved by Jesus' words, asked, "Where are you staying?", he replied, "Come, and you will see." (See John 1:38–39.) Following this example, the Church needs pastors who do not impose or withhold, but accompany. Who do not block the way, but open it. Who say with their lives, "Come and see."

The Lord Himself Comes to Meet Us

Pope Leo XIV reminds us again and again that the gospel does not age. It does not wear out. It does not lose its strength. It is the living Word that continues to transform lives. And that is why, in his view, each new pastoral year must begin as a renewed encounter with Christ. Not out of custom, but out of need. Not with fear, but with hope. "The Lord himself comes to meet us," he wrote. "He speaks to our hearts and invites us, once again, to be messengers of his peace and sowers of communion."

This is Leo XIV's vision of the Church: a community that does not isolate itself or guard grace as a privilege, but offers it as a gift. A Church that goes out into the world to serve and build fraternity.

Inspired by Psalm 27, Bishop Prevost invited all to listen to that voice echoing in the heart: "'Come,' says my heart, 'seek his face;' your face, LORD, do I seek! Do not hide your face from me" (Psalm 27:8–9).

The Pope then added that such is the love of God—free, faithful, overflowing. A love that always takes the initiative with infinite gentleness, not bursting in or imposing. A love that lets itself be discovered in silence, in stillness, in interior readiness. We must—amid the noise, tension, and fatigue of the world—make space to listen.

The encounter with Christ is not a one-time event or a memory from the past. It is an experience that renews, a call that echoes each day, deep in the heart. Pope Leo XIV has always lived his encounter with Christ this way: as a personal, tangible relationship that gives meaning to everything else.

In the Pope's spirituality, deeply marked by the Word of God and life in community, the Lord coming to meet us is not only a devotional image but also a practical certainty: Christ is present, Christ draws near to us, Christ takes the initiative. And when he comes to meet us, we too are sent out to meet others—without fear and without delay—because the Christian life begins and is renewed in the encounter with the living Christ, who transforms the heart. As Benedict XVI once said, "Being a Christian is not the result of an ethical choice or a lofty idea, but the encounter with an event, a person, which gives life a new horizon and a decisive direction" (*Deus Caritas Est*, 1).

That encounter with the Lord changes us, moves

us, commits us. It does not leave us indifferent. When someone has heard the Lord call him or her by name, one cannot go on living just any way they please. One discovers that faith is not a refuge for difficult times, but a mission for everyday life.

From there springs the urgency of communion. The Church is an open family, where every person has a place and all are called to build bridges. To be "sowers of communion" is more than a beautiful phrase: it is a way of life; a way of being in the world; a way of speaking, seeing, and acting. In a time wounded by division and indifference, the Church is called to be a sign of unity, a space of reconciliation, a workshop of peace, and a school of truth.

But that mission does not arise from our own strength. It arises from having made room for God, from having listened to him in silence, and from having recognized that he sought us first. As in the story of Emmaus, the Lord walks beside us even when we do not recognize him; he allows himself to be seen when we break the bread and open our hearts.

That is why there is such emphasis on prayer—not as just another obligation, but as the place where the Word becomes alive in us, where we learn to see like Jesus, to listen like Jesus, to love like Jesus. Without that daily encounter in prayer, we risk speaking about God without having heard him, proclaiming the gospel without having lived it. We would be working for him, but without him.

Only from that place—from the wonder of knowing we have been found—can we joyfully proclaim that the Lord is alive and comes to meet us. Again and again. Always.

Suffering Can Lead to Revelation

During the pandemic, when everything seemed uncertain, Bishop Prevost witnessed the deep need for concrete hope. "God's call may seem untimely in the eyes of the world," he said, "but it is more urgent than ever." That is why he proclaimed that suffering, too, can be a place of revelation. That even a pandemic can become, through faith, a *kairos*: a favorable time to return to God and to proclaim him with renewed fervor.

For this reason, Leo XIV evoked the prophetic proclamation of St. John the Baptist: "Behold, the Lamb of God, who takes away the sin of the world" (John 1:29). And he recalled Jesus' unbreakable promise: "In the world you will have trouble, but take courage, I have conquered the world" (John 16:33).

From there, the invitation was clear: to begin each pastoral season as a true reunion with Jesus. With renewed joy. With humble faith. With missionary resolve. To proclaim the gospel not as obligation, but as joy; not as theory, but as shared life. Because if Jesus has conquered sin, death, and every shadow, how can we not proclaim him? How can we remain silent? How can we hide the light, even in the darkest hour?

Robert Prevost made it clear that today, more than ever, it is time to set out and rediscover the beauty of faith, the vitality of the Word, and the strength of the risen One who continues to walk with us. It is time for a Church that listens, that goes out into the world to be challenged by its suffering, and that responds with love.

Dreaming Together

In full harmony with Pope Francis, the bishop of Chiclayo firmly proclaimed that the Christian response can only come from fraternity, because, as he quoted from paragraph 8 of *Fratelli Tutti*, "no one can face life in isolation."

> *Here we have a splendid secret that shows us how to dream and to turn our life into a wonderful adventure. No one can face life in isolation. We need a community that supports and helps us, in which we can help one another to keep looking ahead. How important it is to dream together.*

Bishop Prevost's dream was, and continues to be as Pope Leo XIV, the dream of Christ: a reconciled world, a fraternal Church, and a community of disciples who give from the love they have received and share it without measure. Because if Pope Leo XIV has made one thing clear from the first words of his papacy, it is that God loves us. God loves everyone. And once that love is received, it changes everything.

In this time marked by fragmentation and individualism, Pope Leo XIV invites us to lift our gaze and recover the transformative power of a shared dream. To dream together is not a naive escape, but a prophetic declaration. It means that we believe another world is possible, because God is already bringing it forth among us. And the kingdom of God is realized wherever men and women recognize one another as brothers and sisters.

Leo XIV's dream is not his own. It is not personal or private. It is God's: a reconciled world in which no one is left out, the forgotten are heard, and love is not the exception, but the norm. But for that dream to become reality, it needs roots: people who commit in a concrete way to walk together and who renounce the principle of "every person for him- or herself."

Christian fraternity is not just an idea; it is the heart of the gospel. As St. Paul wrote, "If [one] part suffers, all the parts suffer with it; if one part is honored, all the parts share its joy" (1 Corinthians 12:26). That is what it means to dream together: to know that we are part of one body, sharing responsibility for a hope that belongs to all of us.

Leo XIV has lived this way from the beginning as missionary, as pastor, and as brother. His leadership has always been synodal and profoundly communal. He knows how to listen, to discern, and to journey with others. He understands that the kingdom of God is not built alone, but built by many hands, united hearts, and intertwined dreams.

Leo XIV is a man accustomed to listening: to God in prayer, to the people in their struggles, and to the world in its groaning. That is why he preaches not only with words but also with a constant attitude of attentiveness and openness. He invites the whole Church to tune in to the ear of the heart and to remain attentive to the cry of wounded humanity. He wants us to listen—as he has learned to do—to the sighs of the poor, the questions of the young, the tears of the discarded, and the silent seeking of those who do not yet know Christ.

In his words and gestures, the Pope reminds us that the Church will be living its faith only if it becomes a community that dreams with eyes wide open, walks at the pace of the forgotten, allows itself to be moved by the suffering of the world, and dares to create spaces of encounter where before there was only distance.

And that dream—so vast, so beautiful—does not arise from human optimism, but from the love of God received and believed. As Pope Leo XIV has said, highlighted at the beginning of this chapter, "God loves us. God loves you all." That certainty changes everything: it breaks down fear, dissolves boundaries, and topples walls. And it sends us out with humility and hope to build a community without exclusions, where all people can find their place, their dignity, their voice. A community that stifles judgment, contempt, and indifference, encouraging instead the fruitful silence that the human heart longs for: the silence that listens, that welcomes, and that makes true encounter possible.

To dream together, then, is not a slogan. It is a gospel pathway of living the faith, building peace, and sowing the seeds of the kingdom. And Leo XIV, with simplicity and conviction, is telling us that this dream is worth the effort and that we are not alone in dreaming it.

Chapter 4

Evil Will Not Prevail

"Do not be conquered by evil,
but conquer evil with good."
Romans 12:21

"Evil will not prevail.
All of us are in God's hands."

A Prophetic Declaration

"Evil will not prevail." These words, spoken clearly and firmly by Leo XIV at the start of his pontificate, are more than spiritual consolation—they are prophetic. In a world shaken by social crises, open warfare, and simmering violence; in a time shaped by technological revolutions, human displacement, and ongoing threats to human dignity, the Pope presents himself not as a distant observer, but as a courageous witness of hope. His hope is deeply rooted in the evangelical certainty that God is stronger than all evil and that history remains in God's hands.

Just as Pope Leo XIII published *Rerum Novarum* in 1891 to respond to the labor question and the challenges of industrial capitalism with a renewed voice of Catholic Social Teaching, Pope Leo XIV's pontificate also arises amid great transformations. Then, it was industrialization. Now, it is cultural fragmentation, the rise of artificial intelligence, the climate crisis, mass migration, and ideological polarization. These issues require more than just analysis, Leo XIV's stance is clear: *evil will not have the last word*.

Two days after his election, the Pope explained to the cardinals why he chose the name Leo XIV. It wasn't a symbolic or anecdotal decision; it was a deliberate path with a pastoral and doctrinal orientation that will deeply shape his pontificate. By choosing the name Leo, he unavoidably evoked Pope Leo XIII, who read the signs of the times at the end of the nineteenth century and offered the Church a solid compass in response to modernity. As the saying goes, *Nomen est omen* ("The name reveals the mission"). In this case, it is a clear declaration of intention.

With this gesture, Leo XIV wanted to make it clear

from the outset that his pontificate would carry forward a Church engaged in dialogue; committed to social justice; attentive to workers, the poor, the displaced, and the marginalized; and especially ready to face today's challenges. In his May 10, 2025, address to the College of Cardinals, he said, "In our own day, the Church offers to everyone the treasury of [its] social teaching in response to another industrial revolution and to developments in the field of artificial intelligence."

This is a pontificate that, like that of his esteemed predecessor, will not merely seek to preserve, but to illuminate and accompany the present. The name Leo XIV is a way of telling the world that the Church will not withdraw into itself but will continue to go forth, to proclaim, to listen, and to build paths of peace and fraternity. In this simple but meaningful act of choosing a name, the Pope has laid the groundwork for what will undoubtedly be a demanding, deeply evangelical pontificate.

Christian Courage

Leo XIV is not a pope who speaks from theory. His pastoral life has been shaped by closeness to those who suffer: in Peru's poor neighborhoods, in the towns of the Diocese of Chiclayo, in Augustinian communities scattered across nearly fifty different countries. He knows that faith does not eliminate, but rather transforms, suffering. And he knows that Christian courage does not mean denying the darkness, but walking with hope through it.

In an August 2024 homily as bishop, reflecting on the prophet Elijah, he said:

Even when we're tired, perhaps suffering deeply, when we feel like Elijah, saying, "Enough, Lord, I can't go on,"—that's when the Lord comes to give us strength and walk with us. Sometimes, he pushes us forward, lifts us up, and says, "Keep walking." One way he tells us to keep walking is when we are gathered in community. Alone, we may not make it. But if we are with our sisters and brothers, if we have friends, if we've learned to form a community where we receive support, encouragement, and comfort, then we recognize, as Jesus promised, that where two or three are gathered in his name, he is truly there among us.

This is not a new way of thinking for the Pope. As he has repeated on various occasions, both in Peru and in Rome, faith is not an escape from suffering, but a path of hope through it. It does not deny pain, but infuses it with meaning. Leo XIV has emphasized that God does not always remove the trials, but he sustains us in them. And the believer's strength comes not only from personal prayer but also from the support of others.

One of Leo XIV's most constant teachings has been about the need to walk together in community, shared responsibility, and mutual support. He wants us to remember that the Christian life is not meant to be lived in isolation—least of all in times of adversity.

We Are Not Alone

We are not alone. This is the core of Pope Leo XIV's message. Even if history seems ruled by fear, hatred, or chaos—God does not and will not abandon his people. His presence becomes visible in the community that prays, that accompanies one another, and that resists evil together. And in that communion, evil loses strength. Because wherever there is love, wherever there is truth, wherever there is fraternity, evil retreats.

Leo XIV is a pope of the margins—not only geographical, but symbolic. He desires a Church with wide horizons: one that does not retreat into comfort, but takes risks on what matters. A Church that defends human rights not out of ideology, but out of fidelity to the gospel. A Church that embraces the dignity of every human being, regardless of origin, status, or story. A Church that believes—truly—that every life matters.

In his first homily as Pope, he proclaimed:

[There] are contexts where it is not easy to preach the gospel and bear witness to its truth, where believers are mocked, opposed, despised, or at best tolerated and pitied. Yet, precisely for this reason, [these] are the places where our missionary outreach is desperately needed. A lack of faith is often tragically accompanied by the loss of meaning in life, the neglect of mercy, appalling violations of human dignity, the crisis of the family, and so many other wounds that afflict our society.

While serving as prefect of the Dicastery for Bishops, he said that the Church's mission is to make God's compassion—not his judgment—visible, and that tenderness is our most urgent prophecy. This goes along with Leo

XIV's insistence that evil will not prevail. Not because it does not exist or does not wound, but because the cross of Christ has revealed that love is stronger than death. And in every gesture of solidarity, tenderness, and justice, the kingdom of God breaks through.

In His Hands

Leo XIV's conviction is that *we are all in God's hands.* We are not lost. We are not accidents. We are held by a God who accompanies, who heals, who forgives, who strengthens. A God who walks with us, especially on the days we feel we can walk no more.

As the Pope also used the words "without fear" more than once at his first *Urbi et Orbi* blessing, echoing the words of Pope St. John Paul II on the day of his election: "Do not be afraid." The world changes, but God remains faithful. The storms may shake us, but we will not sink—because we are anchored in God's love.

Speaking to seminarians, he exclaimed:

The first thing I would say are the words Christ repeated so many times in the gospel: 'Do not be afraid.' The Lord calls, and his call is true. Do not be afraid to say yes. Do not be afraid to at least open your hearts—and, if you want, try to see if the Lord is calling you to religious life, to the Augustinian life, to the priesthood, or to other forms of service in the Church....When I was a novice, an older friar who came to visit us said something that still echoes in me: 'persevere.' We must pray for perseverance because none of us is free from difficult moments—whether we're married, single, or Augustinian. We can't give up at the first difficulty, because—and this is important—we'll never get anywhere in life. Perseverance is a great gift the Lord is ready to give us. But we must learn to receive it and make it part of our life—to be strong. It's one of those gifts that grows over time, through the small trials at the beginning, which help us become stronger, able to carry the cross when it becomes heavier. It is what makes us able to keep going.

In a time so full of despair, Leo XIV reminds the world that faith is not an escape; it is perseverance and commitment. That prayer is not passivity; it is a source of resistance. And that the Church has an urgent mission: to proclaim that yes, evil exists, but *it will not prevail*. Because Christ is risen. And we are, now and always, in his hands.

Sustained by a Faithful Love

The certainty that we are in God's hands is not just consolation or a distraction from suffering; it is a profound conviction that runs through the entire Christian life: nothing—not even pain, failure, or death—can separate us from the faithful love of God. As St. Paul proclaims powerfully in his letter to the Romans: "What will separate us from the love of Christ? Will anguish, or distress, or persecution, or famine, or nakedness, or peril, or the sword?… No, in all these things we conquer overwhelmingly through him who loved us" (Romans 8:35, 37).

Pope Leo XIV takes up this apostolic certainty and offers it to the people of God as a beacon in times of uncertainty. The world changes—sometimes at a pace that feels overwhelming—but God does not withdraw or grow weary. On the contrary, he remains. He remains close, and he remains faithful.

This spiritual anchoring has very concrete consequences. People who believe they are God's hands can live with trust, even in the midst of the storm; they can keep walking, even on shaky ground; and they can forgive, rise, and take risks, because they know they are not alone.

The Pope has repeated many times that faith does not spare us from suffering, but it gives us the certainty of a Presence that does not abandon. During his years as bishop in Peru, he witnessed up-close the pain of communities struck by poverty and violence, but he also saw how their faith sustained them through that silent yet steadfast God who comforts without fanfare and gives strength to those who have none left.

This belief does not spring from mere optimism, but from theological trust that God is greater than evil, stronger than fear, and more faithful than our failures. Saint Augustine, with the wisdom of a convert, put it this way in his *Confessions*: "You upheld me with greater strength than I held myself."

Leo XIV invites us today to reclaim that trust that we are not alone, we are not lost, and we are not doomed to drift. We are sustained, we are seen, and we are accompanied. And if God is our foundation, then everything—even the hardest trials—can be transformed into a path of hope leading to him.

Chapter 5

Jesus, the Good Shepherd

"I am the Good Shepherd. A good shepherd lays down his life for the sheep."

John 10:11

"The risen Christ, the Good Shepherd who laid down his life for God's flock."

A Pastoral Style

"The risen Christ, the Good Shepherd who laid down his life for God's flock." These were among the first words Leo XIV spoke as pope. From the very beginning, he wanted to call to mind one of the most powerful and tender images in the gospel. Jesus is the Good Shepherd not only because he leads but also because he knows each of his own, cares for them, protects them, and is willing to give his life for them. In the title of "good shepherd," much of Leo XIV's spirituality, pastoral approach, and lifelong mission are summed up.

From his early years as an Augustinian friar in Chicago to his missionary work in Trujillo, his episcopacy in Chiclayo, and his service at the Vatican, the image of the Good Shepherd has been Robert Francis Prevost's concrete model for ecclesial life. This image is not an abstract ideal, but a real way of being a shepherd in the midst of the people—a shepherd who listens, is moved by others' suffering, accompanies patiently, and never abandons the wounded.

While serving as prefect in Rome, he said, "A fundamental element of a bishop's identity is to be a shepherd—able to be close to all members of the community, starting with the priests, for whom the bishop is both father and brother. To live this closeness with everyone, without excluding anyone."

Elsewhere, he also said, "Being a good shepherd means being able to accompany the people of God and live near them, not isolated. Pope Francis has made this very clear many times. He does not want bishops who live in palaces. He wants bishops who live in relationship with

God, with other bishops, with priests, and especially with the people of God—in a way that reflects the compassion and love of Christ, building community, learning to live what it means to be part of the Church in an integral way that includes much listening and dialogue."

On several occasions, especially when speaking of the episcopal ministry, he has highlighted the symbol of the crosier, or pastoral staff. Often overlooked, the crosier takes on powerful symbolic value here. That gentle curve at the end of the staff is not ornamental; it is a sign of attentiveness and care, used to gently bring back those who stray, like a shepherd drawing in a lost sheep so that none is left behind. "The bishop must recognize that he is called to serve, to draw near to the people, and to seek out those who are a little lost. I always remember the image of the bishop's pastoral staff, which often has that curved hook, because the bishop must sometimes walk ahead to lead, sometimes walk with the people, and sometimes stay behind to push gently those who are falling behind. Simply put, the bishop must be with the people: listening, knowing their reality, opening his eyes to the suffering of so many people and communities, and doing all he can to be with them, to share faith, and to announce Jesus Christ in the world—and, in this sense, to encourage the people of God with hope wherever he serves."

Being a good shepherd also means being firm at times, such as when supporting the weak or protecting the defenseless. This understanding of pastoral ministry has shaped Leo XIV's formation of priests, closeness to rural communities, and daily involvement in parish life. In an interview with his order, he said, "Thus, the bishop must have many skills. He must know how to govern, administer, organize, and relate to people. But if I had to name one trait above all others, it is this: he must proclaim Jesus Christ and live the faith so that the faithful see in his witness an encouragement to participate more actively in the Church that Christ himself founded. Ultimately, the goal is to help people come to know Christ through the gift of faith."

Jesus Never Abandons His Flock

During his ministry in Peru, Leo XIV's pastoral way of being came alive in his visits to remote communities, celebrations in hard-to-reach places, and constant dialogue with laypeople, religious, and pastoral workers. In a message to the catechists of the Diocese of Chiclayo, he wrote, "Jesus never abandons his flock. And we cannot abandon those entrusted to us. To be a shepherd is to carry others, to walk with them—not from a position of power, but with tenderness."

This pastoral tenderness is not weakness; it is evangelical strength. It is the strength of the one who cares, who watches over, who shows compassion. A good shepherd does not act out of fear or judgment, but out of unconditional love. And that is the Church's calling, too: to reflect the heart of Jesus, the Good Shepherd, in the midst of a fragmented world where so many feel scattered, lost, or rejected.

Leo XIV expressed in his inaugural message that the Church is the flock of God. The Church is also God's home, his school of mercy, and his workshop of communion. We can only be credible witnesses of the gospel if we reflect the heart of the Good Shepherd who knows, tends, and gives his life for his sheep.

In that same spirit, the Pope's pastoral vision insists on a model of the Church that accompanies rather than condemns, that welcomes rather than excludes, that guides without imposing. A Church that draws near—like the shepherd with "the smell of the sheep," as Pope Francis often repeated. Throughout his religious life, Robert Prevost not only has preached this approach but also has lived it among peasants, migrants, the sick, the young, and those who feel they no longer have a place in the Church.

We know that Jesus, the Good Shepherd, not only leads but also seeks out and carries. He comforts and gives his life. In that model, Leo XIV finds his spiritual horizon and his daily task: to reflect in his Petrine ministry not the figure of an administrator or judge, but of a shepherd whose heart is in Christ.

This is what the Pope also asks of all the baptized. In the Church, all of us—each according to his or her vocation—are called to be shepherds to each other by caring for one another, seeking one another out, supporting one another, and loving one another. That is the true face of a synodal, evangelical, and living Church. That is the Church of the Good Shepherd.

THE GOOD SHEPHERD LAYS DOWN HIS LIFE FOR THE SHEEP

"I am the Good Shepherd. A good shepherd lays down his life for the sheep" (John 10:11). In the midst of today's global tensions, marked by war, inequality, loneliness, and mistrust, Pope Leo XIV has chosen to return, as previously mentioned, to one of the oldest and most beloved images of the gospel: Jesus as the Good Shepherd. This image, so familiar to the early Christians and so deeply rooted in the Church's spirituality, is not just a symbol. It is a way of life and a key to understanding the very heart of God and the mission of those who serve Him.

Jesus does not present himself as just any shepherd. He knows his sheep, and they know him. "I am the good shepherd, and I know mine and mine know me, just as the Father knows me and I know the Father; and I will lay down my life for the sheep" (John 10:14–15).

The "knowing" Jesus speaks of is not intellectual, but intimate, tender, and loving. It is the knowing of one who has entered the life of the other, who has become a companion on the way. Jesus does not lead from afar; he is near. He goes ahead to guide, walks alongside to accompany, and stays behind to gather those who have fallen back, just as Leo XIV has emphasized.

This pastoral vision of leadership, in today's terms, resonates deeply with the ancient writings of St. Augustine of Hippo, by whose example Pope Leo XIV is inspired and whose way of thinking the Pope knows well. It is an authority that does not dominate; it accompanies. It is a Church that does not exist for itself; it gives itself in love.

Today, more than ever, following the example of the Good Shepherd is urgent. The Church must reflect that face of Christ: compassionate, attentive, humble, and firm. Every bishop—every Christian—is called to live out this kind of service in the real lives of people: visiting homes, listening to sorrows, celebrating hopes, denouncing injustice, and opening paths of reconciliation.

At heart, being a good shepherd is about living as Jesus lived, with feet dusty from the journey and a heart burning with love. Only then will the shepherd recognize the flock—and, more importantly, will the flock recognize in him the voice of the One True Shepherd.

Chapter 6

To Be Missionaries

"[The disciples] went forth and preached everywhere, while the Lord worked with them and confirmed the word through accompanying signs."

Mark 16:20

"Faithful to Jesus Christ, in order to proclaim the gospel without fear, to be missionaries."

The Gospel Is Proclaimed With Boldness

The gospel is not something to keep—it is something to proclaim. And it is proclaimed not with fear, but with courage; not from comfort, but from commitment; not just to some, but to all.

For more than two decades—exactly twenty-three years—at different times, Robert Francis Prevost was a missionary in Peru: first, in the mission of Chulucanas, Piura (1985-1986), and then in Trujillo, where he served as community prior (1988-1992), director of formation (1988-1998), and instructor of professed friars (1992-1998). In the Archdiocese of Trujillo, he was judicial vicar (1989-1998) as well as a professor of canon law, patristics, and moral theology at the major seminary of San Carlos and San Marcelo.

Later, in 2014, Pope Francis appointed Prevost as apostolic administrator of the Diocese of Chiclayo (Peru) and bishop of the titular Diocese of Sufar, for which Prevost was ordained on December 12, the feast of Our Lady of Guadalupe. He was then appointed as bishop of Chiclayo in September 2015. In this role, he was a firsthand witness to poverty, social violence, and institutional abandonment—as well as to the living faith of the people, the solidarity of the communities, and the transforming power of the gospel. His time as bishop of Chiclayo, from 2015 until 2023, profoundly shaped his spirituality and his vision of the Church.

Pope Leo XIV constantly insists that all pastoral renewal must begin from a single source: the encounter with Jesus Christ. As he has often written in his letters and preached in his homilies, we must know Jesus to make him known, and we must live in communion with him to be able to proclaim him authentically. On various occasions, the Pope has emphasized that the gospel is not a set of ideas, rules, or rituals. It is a living person. And once people meet that person, they cannot keep him to themselves.

Pope Leo XIV defines the core of the Christian mission by affirming that proclaiming the gospel is not about spreading a doctrine, but about sharing an experience. To evangelize is to bear witness to an encounter that has changed one's life. It is to speak not so much of "something," but of "someone." Jesus is not a figure of the past, nor an abstract model, but a real presence who walks with us, transforms us, and sends us forth.

> *Though today's society appears increasingly secularized and unbelieving, the Church's great challenges have not changed in two thousand years. The mission Christ entrusted to his disciples remains: "Go, therefore, and make disciples of all nations, baptizing them in the name of the Father, and of the Son, and of the Holy Spirit, teaching them to observe all that I have commanded you" (Matthew 28:19–20). This is the root of all missionary activity and the heart of the evangelical mandate that never loses relevance, no matter the cultural or technological shifts. Beyond the cultural, linguistic, or social differences that shape the world's communities, the Church faces one and the same challenge: to proclaim Jesus Christ and extend his gospel.*

During his time as prior general of the Augustinians, he learned to live and value the catholicity of the Church: its universality, the diversity of its faces, and the richness of its contexts. "Italy, Spain, the United States, Peru, or China, for example, may have very different pastoral priorities, but all share the same call: to bring the gospel into every corner of the human heart. The challenge does not change, even if the methods do. The key is to balance fidelity and creativity: fidelity to the eternal message of the gospel, and pastoral creativity to announce it in a way that is understandable, incarnate, and close to each specific context."

"To recognize the diversity of the people of God," he said, "is not an obstacle, but an opportunity to enrich the mission. It helps us reach people more effectively and respond with greater sensitivity and strength to what the Church is called to today."

In short, what is essential remains unchanged: Jesus Christ is still the center, and the proclamation of his kingdom is the Church's most urgent task. Languages will change, strategies will change, and contexts will change, but the Good News is always the same, and it still needs courageous witnesses who live it and share it with joy.

The proclamation of the gospel begins, then, in the life of the believer. It is not about having all the answers or imposing rules—it is about having been touched by the love of Christ and wanting others to know him too. It is a natural response to the joy of knowing that oneself is loved and saved.

Leo XIV, following in the footsteps of Pope Francis and so many evangelizers with humble hearts, insists that the Church must recover the freshness of the first proclamation of the Good News—the *kerygma*, as the apostles called it. As Pope Francis highlighted, "Jesus Christ loves you; he gave his life to save you; and now he is living at your side every day to enlighten, strengthen, and free you" (*Evangelii Gaudium*, 164).

From this perspective, evangelization is not a task reserved for a few; it is the vocation of every baptized person. Every Christian is called to be a bearer of hope, a messenger of the Good News that must be shared. Leo XIV has lived this from the beginning of his missionary vocation in Peru, crossing mountains and rivers by horseback or mule to reach remote areas where Christ had not yet been proclaimed. He did not arrive with polished speeches, but with friendship, readiness to listen, and the conviction that Christ is alive and wants to encounter everyone.

When the gospel is proclaimed truthfully, it awakens freedom. It does not oppress, control, or crush; it liberates, uplifts, and heals. Remember, the gospel is not an ideology or a system of ethics; it is the personal love of God, who seeks each of us by name and allows us to respond to him freely.

When someone has received that love, he or she cannot help but share it. Think of the disciples on the road to Emmaus, who, after recognizing Jesus in the breaking of the bread, ran back to announce him. So too, says Leo XIV, we are called to live as a Church that walks, encounters, and proclaims.

Social Justice and Human Rights

Mission cannot be separated from justice. In Peru, marked by deep inequalities and historical wounds, Leo XIV defended human rights firmly, especially during times of social unrest. He facilitated dialogue, denounced violence and corruption, and consistently worked to ensure that the Church remained a space of welcome, peace, and dignity. In 2020, amid the country's political and health crisis, he wrote, "As a Church, we cannot remain on the sidelines of the people's suffering. Our mission is to proclaim Christ, yes—but also to defend life, care for the poor, and protect the vulnerable. The gospel demands justice."

His commitment was not ideological, but evangelical. He was not seeking prominence, but coherence with the faith. In every gesture, he tried to show that mission is not limited to verbal proclamation; it includes the transformative action of charity and justice.

From his first days as pope, Leo XIV expressed deep concern for the injustices that afflict the most vulnerable, drawing inspiration from Pope Leo XIII. In his first meeting with cardinals after the conclave, he emphasized the importance of continuing the spiritual legacy of Pope Francis, especially Francis' example of dedication to the most vulnerable and his bold engagement with the contemporary world.

Another of Leo XIV's pastoral priorities is the situation of migrants. Archbishop Gustavo García-Siller of San Antonio, Texas, publicly expressed hope that the Pope would be a strong voice in defending the dignity of those forced to leave their homeland. This perspective—deeply rooted in the gospel—reflects continuity with the

Church's social doctrine, which does not seek to impose solutions, but to accompany processes and respond to current challenges with faithful creativity.

Attention to the Peripheries

Prevost's Latin American experience gave him a deep sensitivity to the peripheries—both geographic and existential. He often visited the most remote communities, celebrated with farmers, listened to migrants, and spoke with young people and families struck by poverty. But, for him, there are no "peripheral" places in the heart of the Church; everyone is at the center when they are loved by Christ.

In harmony with Pope Francis, Leo XIV has insisted that the future of the Church runs through these peripheries. There, faith is renewed, vision is purified, and the sense of mission is rekindled. During a visit to a rural parish, Leo stated that no place is too far to deserve a shepherd, and no one is too broken to be embraced by the gospel.

With such words, Pope Leo XIV has drawn one of the guiding lines of his pontificate: attention to the peripheries, just like his predecessor. But he refers not only to geographically distant places. Above all, he means those human realities that are often ignored or marginalized: loneliness, silent suffering, poverty, doubt, sin, despair.

The Church's mission cannot be limited to safe or predictable spaces. The true gospel, as Pope Francis has already affirmed, plays out in the street, in real encounters with those left behind. Leo XIV, whose pastoral sensibility was deeply shaped by his years in Latin America, understands that the peripheries are not only zones of need but also places of revelation. There, the face of Christ is revealed in the faces of the poor, the excluded, the ones who "don't count"—a truth that today's world finds difficult to accept.

During his episcopate in Chiclayo, Bishop Prevost tirelessly visited the most remote rural areas, where the presence of a pastor was experienced as an unexpected blessing. He made himself available to the people in communion and compassion. He proclaimed the gospel with words, but he also provided the quiet, merciful presence that walks alongside, listens, and sustains. That pastoral style, marked by tenderness and fidelity, has accompanied him ever since.

Under Pope Leo XIV's guidance, the Church is called to embrace the peripheries. All human stories—even the ones most marked by wounds or sin—have a place in the heart of God, which means they have a place in the heart of the Church. It is not in power, but in fragility, that the kingdom of God is made manifest. And that is what Leo XIV proclaims with clarity.

He embodies this spirit in a world where many have been wounded—sometimes by social indifference, sometimes by exclusion, and not infrequently by the Church itself. For him, the shepherd does not ask whether someone deserves to be heard or helped. He simply draws near—with the tenderness of Christ, who heals, restores, and gives back dignity. Because the gospel does not fear the dust of the road, and it is not scandalized by human wounds. On the contrary, it is precisely there that its transforming power is revealed.

Without Fear

Mission requires courage, and Robert Francis Prevost has shown this with his life. He has crossed borders, learned languages, and accompanied vastly different realities—cultural, social, spiritual—all the while repeating firmly: "without fear." Fear paralyzes, divides, and silences; faith propels, unites, sends forth, and banishes fear.

That is why Leo XIV's call for us to be missionaries is not just an exhortation or suggestion, but it is the affirmation of a vocation essential to the whole Church. Proclaiming the gospel today means taking risks, going out to meet others, and stepping into discomfort. But it also means opening ourselves to the greatest joy: discovering that Christ walks with us and that with him everything is possible.

"Do not be afraid," Jesus said again and again to his disciples. Today, he repeats it through the voice of Pope Leo XIV, who tirelessly invites the Church to go out, to take risks, to trust. There are no wounds too deep, no peripheries too distant, no injustices too great that God cannot transform. But that transformation begins when his disciples set out—without fear. In his first *Regina Caeli*, Leo XIV implores, "And to young people, I say: 'Do not be afraid! Accept the invitation of the Church and of Christ the Lord!'"

The gospel is not meant to sit securely on shelves or be recited from comfortable places. It is meant to be carried to the frontiers of human suffering, where there is thirst for hope and truth. A courageous faith is what must drive the Church; a faith that does not become trapped behind fear, but that goes out to meet the other across the whole world.

Sometimes the path is uncertain, resources are scarce, and the conditions are hostile, but we are not alone. As Psalm 23:4 reminds us, "Even though I walk through the valley of the shadow of death, I will fear no evil, for you are with me; your rod and your staff comfort me."

Leo XIV began his pontificate with a clear and resolute invitation to the whole Church: do not let yourselves be paralyzed by fear; instead, trust, move forward, embrace. Because God continues to act, continues to call us, and continues to walk with us. He hears the people's cries, and he sees the tears of the forgotten.

And it is here, in the midst of a wounded world, that the Church will rediscover its deepest joy in realizing that the gospel is still Good News for everyone, especially—and above all—for the least of us, God's beloved.

In his homily at the May 9, 2025 *Missa pro Ecclesia* with the cardinals in the Sistine Chapel, Leo XIV emphasized:

> *Even today, there are many settings in which the Christian faith is considered absurd, meant for the weak and unintelligent. Settings where other securities are preferred, like technology, money, success, power, or pleasure. These are contexts where it is not easy to preach the gospel and bear witness to its truth, where believers are mocked, opposed, despised, or at best tolerated and pitied. Yet, precisely for this reason, they are the places where our missionary outreach is desperately needed.*

Always a Missionary

Being a missionary is a permanent vocation that adapts to times and places yet is always defined by proclaiming Christ, serving the people of God, and walking alongside others. In an interview with Vatican journalist Andrea Tornielli, shortly after being named prefect of the Dicastery for Bishops, Archbishop Prevost shared, with simplicity and conviction:

I still consider myself a missionary. My vocation, like that of every Christian, is to be a missionary, to proclaim the gospel wherever one is. Certainly, my life has changed a lot: I have the opportunity to serve the Holy Father, to serve the Church today, here, from the Roman Curia. [It is] a very different mission from before, but also a new opportunity to live a dimension of my life that has always simply meant saying "yes" when asked to serve. With this spirit, I ended my mission in Peru, after eight and a half years as bishop and almost twenty years as a missionary, to begin a new one in Rome.

These words clearly summarize the thread that has run through Leo XIV's life: unconditional availability, serene fidelity to the Lord's call, and a deep understanding that being a missionary is not a function, but an identity. It is not simply a matter of going to a distant country or living in difficult conditions—though he did that for decades—but of living the gospel by continually giving the gift of himself wherever the Church needs him. And that spirit of readiness carried him from the streets of northern Peru to the halls of the Vatican with the same pastoral style.

Throughout his journey, Leo XIV never sought office, but he accepted it with obedience. He never pursued visibility, but he was placed in key roles. He never stopped reminding others that every ministry is, at its heart, a form of mission. And his pastoral style—as bishop, prefect, and now pope—reflects that same conviction: wherever the gospel must be proclaimed, there is mission to be lived. This missionary dimension also shapes his understanding of the Church: a Church that goes forth, as Pope Francis asked—a Church that does not close in on itself but gives itself away.

For Leo XIV, a missionary is someone who not only crosses geographic borders but also, above all, who dares to cross interior boundaries such as fear, prejudice, conformity, and comfort. It is someone who, moved by the gospel, leaves self behind to meet others with humility, respect, and the joy of one who has been touched by grace. Being a missionary is not a role for a few, but a universal call—a vocation that calls us to become a neighbor, extend a hand, and share life with the whole Church.

Shortly before becoming a cardinal, Bishop Prevost affirmed:

> *We must proclaim the Good News of the kingdom of God even as we understand the Church in her universal reality. This is one of the things I learned as prior general of the Augustinians, and it has undoubtedly been a great preparation for the role I now have. There are many different cultures, many*

different languages, many different circumstances throughout the world where the Church is called to respond.

That mission—as ancient as the gospel—is what Leo XIV has wished to proclaim boldly from the very start of his ministry as Successor of Peter, knowing that today, the proclamation of faith must also exist in the new territories of digital culture.

Leo XIV is, in many ways, the pope of a new era: the technological era or, more precisely, the era of artificial intelligence. He will not be swept along by technology without discernment; rather, he will utilize it with evangelical wisdom. Because in every innovation, in every advancement, the same questions still echo: Where is humanity? Where is God? And who will listen to the cries of the least in this hyperconnected—and so often dehumanized—world?

Chapter 7

A Synodal Church

"Keep watch over yourselves and over the whole flock of which the Holy Spirit has appointed you overseers, in which you tend the Church of God that he acquired with his own blood."

Acts 20:28

"To all of you…throughout the world: we want to be a synodal Church, a Church that moves forward."

COMMUNION, LISTENING, AND CONVERSION

Few concepts have gained as much prominence in twenty-first-century ecclesial life as *synodality*. And few have embodied it with such coherence and depth as Robert Francis Prevost, now Pope Leo XIV.

Long before ascending to the papacy, his lived experience as a missionary, pastor, and formator brought him face-to-face with the challenges of a Church called to journey together, to listen to the Spirit, and to discern collectively the path of the gospel. "The Spirit goes before us, overflows our expectations, and calls us to mutual listening," he said as prefect of the Dicastery for Bishops during the 2023 Synod on Synodality in Rome.

In a late-stage interview with *Vatican News* during the Synod, Cardinal Prevost stressed that the process "represents a profound invitation to personal and communal conversion within the Church." He emphasized that the Synod is not simply an assembly, but "a living experience of listening, dialogue, and discernment" and insisted that "to walk together is the very essence of what it means to be a Church."

His ideas flow from a deep theological and spiritual conviction that stretches back to the earliest days of Christianity: the people of God are called to journey in unity, with shared responsibility, in prayer and openness to the Spirit. For Pope Leo XIV, synodality is not a method; it is a way of being. A way of living in ecclesial communion and encounter amid diversity. A prophetic witness to unity in a world torn by division. A Church that listens to the Holy Spirit.

He explained the following in a May 2023 interview

with Vatican Media after becoming the prefect of the Dicastery for Bishops earlier in the year: :

> *I truly believe that the Holy Spirit is very much present in the Church at this moment and is pushing us toward renewal. We are therefore called to a great responsibility—to live what I call a "new attitude." It's not just a process. It's not simply about changing procedures or having more meetings before making a decision. It's much more. And this is also what causes some difficulty, because at the core, we must be able to listen first and foremost to the Holy Spirit and to what he is asking of the Church.*

In the same interview, he offered the following guidance for walking this path:

> *We must be able to listen to one another, to recognize that this isn't about arguing a political agenda or promoting pet issues. Sometimes people reduce everything to a vote to decide what we'll do next. But it's about something much deeper: it's about learning to truly listen to the Holy Spirit and to the spirit of truth-seeking that lives in the Church.*
>
> *We must move from an experience in which authority speaks and that's the end, to one in which we value the charisms, gifts, and ministries within the Church. Episcopal ministry is an important service—yes—but it must be placed at the service of the Church in this synodal spirit, which simply*

means walking together, all of us, and seeking together what the Lord asks of us in this time.

Episcopal Leadership

Leo XIV is a man deeply rooted in the spirit of the Second Vatican Council. He made this evident in his first homily as pope, in which he quoted several conciliar documents and emphasized the centrality of a Church that walks in unity. As we have seen, synodality is not a fad or a strategy for him, but a constitutive dimension of the Church, one that calls for a renewal of episcopal leadership.

The bishop, he affirms, must be first and foremost close to the people—attentive to their real needs, present in their joys and sorrows. "A bishop must be committed to people's suffering," he said, "and willing to share the faith and announce Christ with hope and closeness."

He has reflected on this often, emphasizing that the bishop's role is to be a servant of ecclesial unity, especially in a time marked by tension and polarization. In this light, he has affirmed that the three guiding principles of the synodal process—participation, communion, and mission—form the right path. He said the following in the aforementioned May 2023 Vatican Media interview:

The bishop is called to this charism to live the spirit of communion, to promote unity within the Church and with the pope. This is also what it means to be Catholic, because without Peter, where is the Church?

Jesus prayed "that they may all be one" (John 17:21). And it is this unity that we want to see in the Church. Today, society and culture draw us away from what Jesus wants for us, and that causes great harm. Lack of unity is a wound—a painful wound—for the Church. Division and controversy help no one. We bishops, especially, must accelerate the movement toward unity, toward communion in the Church.

In keeping with this vision, Leo XIV has acknowledged the vital role of episcopal conferences in the synodal journey. Although the structure and context of each conference vary, all are focused on adopting the logic of communion. Some conferences include practices such as "conversation in the Spirit," enabling collective discernment through deep listening and spiritual openness. This dynamic not only strengthens episcopal fraternity but also fosters more faithful and accessible pastoral service to local churches.

Polarization—A Sign of Deeper Wounds?

Before his election as pope, Cardinal Robert Francis Prevost spoke out against polarization both within the Church and in the wider world. In his view, internal divisions are not merely theological or pastoral disagreements; they are symptoms of deeper wounds that reflect broad social, cultural, and ideological tensions. He acknowledged it with clarity: "Polarization is not a phenomenon unique to the Church, but a reality present in many societies."

Yet, he emphasized that the Church cannot afford to reproduce these same dynamics. The Church's mission is the opposite: to become a place of reconciliation, mutual listening, and genuine dialogue. The Christian community is not called to be a space where conflict is stoked, but where people learn to appreciate diversity and build together.

In this context, he has firmly espoused that the synodal process represents a great opportunity. "The synod is an invitation to overcome polarization and to promote spaces of encounter, listening, and mutual understanding in the spirit of the gospel," he has said and reiterated during his participation in the synodal assembly.

When he was made cardinal, he again emphasized that finding harmony in diversity is a challenge:

Especially when polarization has become the default mode in a society that, instead of seeking unity as a fundamental principle, swings from one extreme to another. Ideologies have come to hold more power than the lived experience of humanity, of faith, of the values we embody. Some misunderstand unity as uniformity: "You must be just like us." No. That cannot be.

Nor can we understand diversity as a way of living without criteria or order. That approach overlooks the fact that, from the very creation of the world—the gift of nature, the gift of human life, the gift of so many different things that we actually live and celebrate—none of it can be sustained by inventing my own rules and doing things my own way. These are ideological positions. When ideology becomes, so to speak, the master of my life, then I can no longer engage in dialogue with

> *others, because I've already decided how things must be. And so, I close myself off from encounter, and transformation becomes impossible. That can happen anywhere in the world, about any issue. And, obviously, it makes it very difficult to be a Church, to be a community, to be brothers and sisters.*

For Leo XIV, then, synodality is not a strategy plan or a restructuring plan. It is, above all, a spiritual and ecclesial experience that involves three essential dimensions: **conversion, journey, and horizon**.

Conversion, because it requires a change in attitude—setting aside prejudice, opening oneself to difference, and allowing oneself to be challenged by the voice of the other.

Journey, because it is not a one-time decision or a short-term strategy; to live synodally takes time, intentionality, patience, and communal discernment.

Horizon, because it is not enough to reorganize structures or draft documents; it is about dreaming and building a more evangelical, more open, more fraternal Church.

With his calm, reflective, and deeply pastoral style, Robert Francis Prevost has shown that synodality is not a theory; it is a concrete way of living the gospel today. He lived this way in Peru, accompanying grassroots pastoral care. He lived it in Rome, accompanying the discernment of bishops in a spirit of communion. And now, as Leo XIV, he continues to promote that same spirit from the heart of the universal Church.

"We want to be a synodal Church," he said. "A Church

that walks together, always seeks peace, always seeks charity, always strives to remain close—especially to those who suffer." This is not a rhetorical statement. It is a deep, evangelical, and urgent commitment. It is a vocation. And the synodal path is one we must all take up—a promise of real, possible, and necessary renewal.

Chapter 8

A United Church

"Every day they devoted themselves to meeting together in the temple area and to breaking bread in their homes. They ate their meals with exultation and sincerity of heart."

Acts 2:46

"To walk together with you as a Church, united."

A Brother Among Brothers

"To walk with you as a Church, united" is the clear statement of a pope who presents himself as a brother among brothers and as a pastor in the midst of his people. He reaffirms from the outset his commitment to unity, to communion, and to a Church that walks together in diversity. In times marked by fragmentation, exclusionary rhetoric, and the temptation to retreat into identity-based isolation, this affirmation is both a spiritual proposal and a pastoral program.

For Robert Francis Prevost, this conviction did not begin with the start of his pontificate; it has been a constant in his life. At his episcopal ordination, he chose as his motto words from St. Augustine that reveal the heart of his spirituality: *In illo uno unum* ("In the One, we are one"). This expression, taken from St. Augustine's commentary on Psalm 127 in *Enarrationes in Psalmos* (Expositions on the Psalms), distills an essential insight of the bishop of Hippo: "Though we are many, in the One we are one" (*Nos multi in illo uno unum*).

By choosing this motto, Bishop Prevost wanted to express that the episcopal ministry is radically at the service of communion. The bishop is not a supervisor or a soloist, but a craftsman of unity. The Church is not built on personal interests or agendas, but on shared belonging to Christ, in whom all—despite our differences—are made one.

In an interview with Vatican Media in July 2023, then-Cardinal Prevost explained this conviction clearly: "As my episcopal motto reflects, unity and communion are part of the charism of the Order of Saint Augustine and also of my way of acting and thinking. I believe it is essential to promote communion in the Church, and we know well that communion, participation, and mission are the three key words of the synod. Therefore, as an Augustinian, promoting unity and communion is fundamental. Saint Augustine speaks frequently about unity in the Church and the need to live it."

That unity does not mean uniformity. Leo XIV knows this well. His own life—shaped by community, missionary experience, and ecclesial leadership—has taught him that true communion is built on mutual listening, respect for differences, and the centrality of Christ as the bond of unity. In him, and only in him, can a truly Catholic Church be founded: universal, open, and welcoming.

> *One must be "Catholic" above all. Sometimes a bishop runs the risk of focusing only on the local dimension. But a bishop needs a much broader vision of the Church...and must experience the universality of the Church. He must also have the ability to listen to others and ask for advice, as well as psychological and spiritual maturity. A fundamental element of the bishop's profile is to be a pastor—capable of being close to members of the community, starting with the priests, for whom the bishop is both father and brother. To live this closeness to all, without excluding anyone.*

That is why, as pope, he has retained the same motto on his coat of arms: *In illo uno unum.* He did this not out of habit or tradition, but as an explicit sign of continuity.

The coat of arms speaks of his identity; the motto, of his mission. It is a way of saying that unity is not a slogan for speeches, but a daily task requiring humility, patience, discernment, and prayer.

To walk together as a united Church is the very heart of the synodal path. It is the concrete way for the Church to be faithful to the gospel in our time. It is how we listen to the Spirit, who always comes upon us where there is openness, communion, and readiness.

Leo XIV knows this, lives it, and proposes it to all of us. He invites us all—bishops, priests, consecrated men and women, and laypeople—not to resign ourselves to a divided or polarized Church, but to actively commit to building a real communion that is the living witness of the love of Christ that gathers us together and sends us forth.

Living in Communion

As we've previously said, and as Leo XIV has stressed time and again, unity is not uniformity. Unity does not mean thinking the same, feeling the same, or acting the same. It means living in communion, in reciprocal listening, in mutual charity. And that requires deep roots.

That is why this Augustinian pope has so often insisted on the Eucharist as "the source and summit of the Christian life." Because in the Eucharist we learn to live as family—not by human effort, but by the gift received. In the Eucharist, we do not simply celebrate a mystery; we learn a way of life.

In one of his homilies as bishop of Chiclayo, he said, "Communion is not imposed. It is built. It is lived. And it flows from…Christ—given, broken, risen. Without the

Eucharist, there is no Church. And without community, there is no living gospel."

This ecclesial vision has not changed with the passing of years or with the responsibilities he has received; on the contrary, it has deepened. As prefect of the Dicastery for Bishops, he repeatedly insisted that the Church needs pastors who foster unity, who reject clericalism, and who know how to value each charism in the people of God. Unity is not built from power, but from humility, service, and listening.

We know that, in full harmony with Pope Francis, Pope Leo XIV champions a synodal Church, where we all walk together, no one is left behind, and everyone is heard. And for that to be possible, unity must be a living experience embodied in parishes, in dioceses, in religious communities, in every daily gesture of communion.

Saint Augustine himself expressed it clearly: "Be one, be one in Christ. Not in yourselves, but in him. Not from your own strength, but from his grace. Because if we are divided, we are not his body."

This is how Bishop Prevost understood his mission as bishop. This is how Pope Leo XIV understands his mission as Pope. To walk together, to heal the wounds of division, to build bridges, and to invite everyone to the Lord's table without exclusion or condemnation. Because the Church will only be faithful to the gospel if it is a home for all—a visible sign of the unity that God desires to give the world.

Today, more than ever, humanity needs witnesses of this communion. And the Church must remember that its strength does not lie in numbers, nor in organizational structures, nor in social prestige. Its strength lies in unity lived as gift, as task, as vocation. Because Jesus prays in the Gospel of John "that they may all be one, as you, Father, are in me and I in you" (John 17:21). This is Christ's prayer. And this, at heart, is also the prayer of Pope Leo XIV: that we may be one. In Christ. With Christ. For the world.

CHAPTER 9

A CHURCH THAT BUILDS BRIDGES

"Through him was life, and this life was the light of the human race."

JOHN 1:4

"To build bridges through dialogue and encounter."

BETWEEN THE HUMAN AND THE DIVINE

"The world needs [Christ's] light. Humanity needs him as the bridge that can lead us to God and his love. Help us, one and all, to build bridges through dialogue and encounter, joining together as one people, always in peace."

These words, spoken by Leo XIV in his first public message, before his *Urbi et Orbi* blessing, summarize one of the deepest insights of his pastoral vision: the Church does not exist to build walls or reinforce trenches, but to build bridges. Bridges between people, cultures, generations, and nations. Bridges between wounds and hopes, between sin and grace, between the human and the divine. The Church is called to be a living bridge, not a checkpoint; a place of encounter, not exclusion.

Pope Leo XIV's conviction was not born on the balcony of Saint Peter's—it has been cultivated throughout the pastoral life of Robert Francis Prevost. He has always insisted that only dialogue, sincere listening, and genuine encounter can lead to authentic reconciliation. It is not about enforcing uniformity or negotiating truth; it is about opening pathways where there is mistrust or distance.

In one of his pastoral writings as bishop of Chiclayo, he clearly stated that as men and women of faith, we cannot live in isolation. No one lives his or her faith alone; no one is saved alone. Faith is always ecclesial. Faith draws us toward others. Faith makes us brothers and sisters. Every message of faith, therefore, is a message of unity; we cannot live a faith without charity, without solidarity, without community.

These words are not theory or rhetoric—they come from lived encounter. Leo XIV knows, because he has experienced it firsthand, that a Church that closes in on itself fades away. And a Church that goes out, takes risks, and engages in dialogue is a living, missionary Church.

Recognizing One Another as Brothers and Sisters

Pope Francis emphasized from the beginning of his pontificate, and Pope Leo XIV takes up with the same evangelical passion, that the world does not need cold doctrines or defensive positions, but witnesses who live the joy of the gospel with others, not against them. It is essential that we rediscover each other, recognize each other as brothers and sisters, and build from our shared dignity. Leo XIV has drawn from that same well to promote a Church unafraid of dialogue, even with those who think or live differently.

This mutual recognition is a deeply Christian conviction. We are children of the same Father and, therefore, brothers and sisters. From this certainty, Leo XIV promotes a Church that does not build barriers or apply labels, but goes out to meet people with open arms, convinced that the other—whoever he or she may be—is never an enemy, but is a brother or sister to discover, a story to hear, a face to welcome.

The gospel is not imposed; it is offered with tenderness, witnessed with integrity, and shared with respect. And so, it is necessary to look at others not with suspicion or judgment, but with compassion. Leo XIV has been clear: the Christian is called to serve and care for the world with humility, especially where human dignity is wounded or denied.

Recognizing each other as brothers and sisters also means overcoming internal divisions, both within and outside the Church. One cannot proclaim the God of love while harboring exclusionary attitudes, feeling resentment, or scorning those who are different. Community is not optional—it is the hallmark of the kingdom that Jesus came to announce; it is the very heart of the Christian message.

"Our priority must be to live the Good News, to live the gospel, to share the enthusiasm that can be born in our hearts and lives when we truly discover who Jesus Christ is," Leo XIV emphasized a few years ago. He shares his conviction that the truth of the gospel becomes visible when it is embodied in a community that lives the new commandment of love: [Jesus said,] "I give you a new commandment: love one another. As I have loved you, so you also should love one another. This is how all will know that you are my disciples, if you have love for one another" (John 13:34–35).

In a world wounded by distrust, discrimination, and exclusion, Pope Leo XIV invites us to walk together, to break out of isolation, and to build bridges. Because wherever two or more recognize each other in communion, the face of the kingdom begins to shine through.

This mutual recognition of our brothers and sisters in Christ is a gospel imperative. Leo XIV understands that fraternity does not arise from sympathy or from cultural or ideological similarities, but from the radical truth that we are all children of the same God. Therefore, every human encounter is an opportunity to discover—or rediscover—that original unity so often forgotten, denied, or wounded.

To recognize one another as brothers and sisters means seeing the other not as a threat or a rival, but as a gift. It requires learning to live with differences, not allowing them to become barriers. It demands healing past wounds, overcoming old prejudices, and dismantling bias. And this begins in the heart: only someone who knows he or she is loved can welcome the other as a brother or sister.

To build bridges means to intentionally build community, invest in the common good, and live reconciled relationships. It means getting involved in others' stories, taking on their pain, rejoicing in their victories, and walking by their side. It is a way of resisting self-centeredness and exclusion and of making the kingdom visible where it once seemed impossible.

To Heal, to Share, to Grow, to Be Enlightened

"The joy Jesus Christ brings to the world—the true joy, not just a fleeting or superficial feeling—is a response of faith and fraternity; it is God's call to heal the wounds of those who suffer, to share from our poverty with those who have less, to grow in the wisdom of God's word, and to let ourselves be enlightened by the Lord, by Jesus, the Word made flesh, who dwelled among us (See John 1:14)," Robert Francis Prevost once said.

To heal, to share, to grow, to be enlightened: four verbs that sketch the profile of a Church not defined by limits or barriers, but by its capacity to give. A Church that responds with compassion, not harshness. A Church that sits at the table with everyone, as its Lord did. A Church that speaks through its life.

Building bridges is not easy. It requires giving up the

pride of always wanting to be right. It demands patience, humility, listening, and availability. It requires time and trust. But it is also the most evangelical thing we can do. Everything in Jesus was and is a bridge: his Incarnation, his cross, his forgiveness, his body given for us. Everything in him is renewal.

Therefore, a Church faithful to the gospel can be nothing other than a Church of encounters, of healing words, of gestures that unite; a Church that is not afraid to touch the wounds of the world; a Church that does not live for itself, but for others; and a Church that knows that in every face, there is a new possibility of meeting God.

This is how Pope Leo XIV lives, and he invites us to live this way too. Because today, more than ever, the world needs bridges. And if the Church wants to remain salt and light, it must be at the forefront of that patient yet unstoppable construction.

For Leo XIV, the Church is not a mosaic of fragments, but a living body learning to integrate diversity without fear, without anxiety, without forced uniformity. The bridges he proposes are not shortcuts or easy compromises, but solid paths where truth and mercy embrace. Wherever there are open wounds, ancient divides, or instances of exclusion, Leo XIV sees an opportunity to build bridges of trust, empathy, and hope.

An example of this can be found in his first *Regina Caeli*:

> *I carry in my heart the sufferings of the beloved Ukrainian people. May everything possible be done to reach an authentic, just, and lasting peace*

as soon as possible. Let all the prisoners be freed and the children return to their families. I am deeply saddened by what is happening in the Gaza Strip; may there be an immediate ceasefire! May humanitarian aid be provided to the stricken civil population, and let all hostages be freed.... I have welcomed with satisfaction the announcement of the ceasefire between India and Pakistan, and I hope that through the upcoming negotiations, a lasting accord may be reached soon.

Church Called to Be Home

A key to the vocation of building bridges is the rediscovery of hospitality as an essential trait of the Church's identity. The Church is called to be a home, not a fortress; an open door, not a watchtower. In a time when cultural, social, and even religious differences seem to erect insurmountable walls, Pope Leo XIV invites us to cultivate a spirituality of welcome that is capable of seeing in each person a summons to encounter. It is not about abandoning Christian identity, but about making it fruitful through dialogue and compassion.

In this same spirit, Leo XIV has highlighted the importance of local communities as places where such bridges are tested and lived. Whether in parishes, schools, community initiatives, or mission outposts, the Church can become a true facilitator of reconciliation. It is there, in the small things, where healing bonds are woven and where fraternity takes on a face. Every gesture—however simple, however subtle—is gathered by God and transformed into good for the world. In the gospel, great changes are born from small things: a grain of wheat, a mustard seed, a cup of water, a gesture of compassion. This is how God works—in the humble, the everyday, the unseen. And this is the aspect of the kingdom that Pope Leo XIV wants to place at the center: not spectacle, but fidelity; not lofty words, but love in action.

Building bridges also requires a deep interior life. One cannot truly engage in dialogue without prayer. One cannot truly listen without silence. One cannot heal without first having been healed. That is why Leo XIV embraces the spirituality of building bridges, which is an open, humble, and patient interior life; a willingness to learn from others; and an ability to carry others' fragility without judgment. This is a spirituality that does not dwell in conflict; rather, it walks through conflict in search of communion.

Leo XIV believes the Church cannot wait for the world to change in order to act; the Church must itself become the change it proclaims. Every bridge built is a rally against isolation and indifference. And every community that chooses to open itself to others—even when it's difficult, even when it hurts—becomes a sign of the kingdom already among us.

Chapter 10

Mary Walks With Us

"And Mary kept all these things, reflecting on them in her heart."
Luke 2:19

"Our Mother Mary always wants to walk at our side."

Filial Trust

From the very beginning, Leo XIV expressed his filial trust in the Virgin Mary. This is a theological, pastoral, and deeply personal affirmation, rooted in his spiritual life and his experience as a missionary, formator, and pastor.

Augustinian spirituality, which shaped Leo's vocation from a young age, presents Mary not as a passive or distant figure, but as a believer, a faithful disciple, and the mother of the Church. In her, we see a model of attention to the Word, free obedience, and active contemplation. Mary does not observe history from the outside; she inhabits it with courage.

During his mission in Peru, Bishop Prevost lived this Marian trust among the people. In homilies, celebrations, and pastoral encounters, he often invoked Mary as a "close mother," "companion on the journey," and "maternal presence among a suffering people." Many communities wounded by poverty rely on the Virgin as a source of comfort and hope. And he, as pastor, shared and nourished that certainty.

As bishop of Chiclayo, he would often say that when the path becomes difficult, when we do not know where to go, when faith feels fragile, Mary takes us by the hand. She does not walk ahead of us; she walks beside us as mother, sister, and companion.

Leo XIV's trust in Mary is a concrete way of living the faith; it is a confident surrender into the hands of the Mother. It is a heart-centered relationship that has accompanied him through the decisive moments of his life and continues to do so now, in his role as Successor of Peter. In Mary, he has always found consolation, inspiration, and strength. Especially in contexts marked by pain, uncertainty, or violence, he understands that Marian devotion is not escape; rather, it is fruitful refuge that sustains the people's hope.

For Leo XIV, Mary is a real woman, deeply human and deeply faithful, and a master of gospel living. She teaches us to listen with the heart, to seek God's will in the everyday, and to say "yes," even in the midst of confusion. That is why his relationship with Mary is not limited to occasional prayers; it is a true devotion.

From his earliest moments as pope, the Marian aspect of Leo XIV's life has been evident. One of his first public acts was a silent prayer before an image of the Virgin. A simple gesture, without fanfare, but with deep significance: to begin his pontificate under the protection of the Mother. Further, in a time of noise, he chose to begin with silence, reminding us that every mission in the Church begins in contemplation.

Mary Inspires Discipleship

Closeness with the Blessed Mother is not separate from mission. On the contrary, Mary inspires discipleship. She was the first disciple, the first to go in haste to serve—as Scripture tells us in its account of the visitation—the first to believe that God could change history through the humble. For this reason, for Leo XIV, Mary is not only refuge, but motivation; not only comfort, but impetus.

In the documents of the diocesan synod that Bishop Prevost led in Chiclayo, he presented Mary as a model of synodality: a woman who listens, who engages in dialogue, who stands at the foot of the cross, who accompanies the birth of the Church. As Leo XIV said during his first *Regina Caeli*, "May the Virgin Mary, whose entire life was a response to the Lord's call, always accompany us in following Jesus."

This understanding of Mary deeply connects with the spirituality of the Latin American people, in which the Virgin is mother, home, comfort. Bishop Prevost learned this in Trujillo, in the processions of Our Lady of Peace, Our Lady of Mount Carmel, and Our Lady of Guadalupe. And he now carries that experience to the heart of the universal Church.

Mary does not impose; she transforms. And she teaches the Church to do the same: to be a mother, a disciple, and a home.

Mary and Synodality

In this light, Leo XIV proposes a synodality with a Marian face. Mary teaches us to walk together in diversity, to build communion through mutual listening, and to sustain others when they falter. Her pedagogy—simple and strong—becomes a model for the entire Church.

In a world wounded by immediacy, self-centeredness, and division, Mary teaches the art of patience, of caring, and of connection. She keeps the presence of God among the people, and her own presence inspires the Church to open itself, welcome, and accompany.

Pope Leo XIV does not keep Marian devotion in the personal realm. He elevates it as an ecclesial dynamism. Mary is comfort, yes, but she is also prophecy. She is mother, but she is also disciple and witness. Leo XIV sees her as a profoundly ecclesial and pastoral model of the Church: selective in words, rich in gestures, quiet but firm, available to listen, and with the strength to support.

THE POPE ENTRUSTS HIMSELF TO MARY

Leo XIV has entrusted his pontificate to the Virgin Mary as an act of trust. He knows that the Church, without Mary's tenderness, risks becoming hardened. That without her quiet strength, it could lose its way. And that without her intercession, it might forget the heart of the gospel.

That is why he invites us to walk with her. Because wherever a mother walks, the journey is never solitary. And in her presence—faithful and constant—the Church finds comfort, direction, and renewed hope.

Conclusion

A Pontificate with Roots and a Future

The pontificate of Pope Leo XIV, Robert Francis Prevost, presents itself as a faithful continuation and courageous deepening of the legacy of his predecessors—especially Pope Francis. His choice of the name "Leo" is no accident: it directly evokes Leo XIII, the great architect of *Rerum Novarum*, and clearly signals a commitment to social justice and engagement with the contemporary world through the lens of the gospel. In his own words, it is about "proclaiming the gospel with eyes fixed on Christ and feet grounded in the soil of history."

From the beginning of his Petrine ministry, Leo XIV has shown that he does not intend to be a pope of grand gestures, but of evangelical depth. In his first homily, delivered on May 9, 2025, in the Sistine Chapel, he declared with conviction that Jesus Christ is "the one Savior who alone reveals the face of the Father." He emphasized that the Church is called to be "a city set on a hill, an ark of salvation sailing through the waters of history, and a beacon that illumines the dark nights of this world." And not because of the splendor of its structures, but because of the "holiness of its members" —men and women transformed by the gospel.

Throughout his journey before the papacy—as an Augustinian friar, as a missionary in the northern regions of Peru, as bishop of Chiclayo, and later as the prefect of the Dicastery for Bishops—he has cultivated a pastoral style marked by closeness, discernment, and mercy. His experience in Latin America has deeply sensitized him to the peripheries, both geographic and existential, and convinced him that it is there—in the fragile—that the face of Christ is most powerfully revealed.

With the gospel as his foundation, his voice rises with clarity against inequality, violence, forced migration, and all forms of exclusion. For Leo XIV, social justice is not an ancillary pastoral concern, but a core component of the Church's mission. These powerful words written during his ministry in Peru bear repeating: "Our mission is to proclaim Christ, yes, but also to defend life, care for the poor, and protect the vulnerable. The gospel demands justice."

Another essential axis of his pontificate is synodality. Leo XIV has insisted that the Church cannot be fragmented or polarized but must move forward as one body in which all the baptized—religious and laypeople alike—listen to each other in authentic communal discernment. He has affirmed that the bishop must be a facilitator of communion and a promoter of unity, living a spirituality of service rather than of power. His episcopal and papal motto, drawn from St. Augustine—*In illo uno unum*—expresses this vision clearly: "In the One, we are one." Because only in Christ is a truly reconciled and missionary Church possible.

In his inaugural homily, he asked his brother cardinals to walk with him in this demanding mission, which he described as a cross, but also as a blessing. And he did so from a posture of humility—not as one who demands, but as one who asks for help in order to serve better. This gospel-rooted style of leadership will undoubtedly be one of the hallmarks of his pontificate.

With Mary, Mother of the Church, to whom he entrusted his ministry from the very beginning, as his companion on the journey, and with the deep conviction that evil will not prevail, Leo XIV invites all the baptized to live their faith with authenticity, joy, and readiness. To live a shared, not a closed, faith; to be a community of missionary disciples, not a self-referential institution.

His first *Urbi et Orbi* blessing, his first *Regina Caeli*, his silent prayer before Mary's image, and his insistent message that the world needs bridges instead of walls are just a few of the clear signs marking his path: a Church that listens, that accompanies, that builds fraternity. A Church that is not afraid of the challenges posed by artificial intelligence, digital culture, or globalization—because it knows that the gospel remains Good News even in our time.

The first North American and Augustinian pope faces many challenges ahead, but his foundation is solid: deep formation, a missionary life lived among the poor, fidelity to prayer, and a spirituality forged in community. As a son of St. Augustine, he knows that the soul is shaped in the encounter with God and with others and that only love transforms the world.

Echoing his spiritual model, he could say to all of us, in words that remain timeless:

> *"Love and do what you will. If you are silent, be silent with love; if you speak, speak with love; if you correct, correct with love; if you pardon, pardon with love. Let love be rooted in you, and from that root nothing but good can grow."*

Saint Augustine,
In Epistolam Ioannis ad Parthos tractatus decem
(Ten Homilies on the Epistle of John to the Parthians), Tract. 7, 8

ABOUT THE AUTHOR

Sr. Gemma Morató Sendra, OP, is a Dominican Sister of Charity of the Presentation of the Blessed Virgin. She was born in Reus, Tarragona, Spain, in 1972. She holds a PhD in humanities from the International University of Catalonia (UIC); a bachelor's degree in moral theology from the Faculty of Theology of Catalonia (FTC); and an advanced specialization in the theology of religious life from the Theological Institute of Religious Life (ITVR) and the Pontifical University of Salamanca (UPSA). She also holds degrees in journalism from Pompeu Fabra University (UPF) and special education from Blanquerna-Ramon Llull University (URL).

She has taught at the Faculty of Communication and International Relations at Blanquerna-Ramon Llull University (URL) since 1999 and has been a tenured professor at the Don Bosco Higher Institute of Religious Sciences (ISCR Don Bosco), affiliated with the Pontifical Salesian University (UPS) in Rome, since 1998. She also teaches at Domuni Universitas, an international online university of the Dominican Order, and at the Institute for Research and Religious Studies of Lleida (IREL).

She is a member of the Blanquerna Observatory on Communication, Religion, and Culture and directs the Mary, Queen of Peace Project—a university residence and meeting center—both in Barcelona. She is also the webmaster for her congregation, which is present in thirty-eight countries around the world.

A columnist in various religious publications, including *Vida Religiosa*, *Vida Nueva*, *Foc Nou*, *Religión Digital*, and others, she has also published several books, especially on religious life and communication.

www.ingramcontent.com/pod-product-compliance
Lightning Source LLC
LaVergne TN
LVHW041632070426
835507LV00008B/571